Coming Back

THE SCIENCE OF REINCARNATION

Based on the Teachings of
His Divine Grace

A. C. BHAKTIVEDANTA
SWAMI PRABHUPĀDA

Founder-*Ācārya* of the International Society
for Krishna Consciousness

THE BHAKTIVEDANTA BOOK TRUST
LOS ANGELES • STOCKHOLM • MUMBAI • SYDNEY

Readers interested in the subject matter of this book are invited by the International Society for Krishna Consciousness to correspond with its Secretary at one of the following addresses:

International Society for Krishna Consciousness
P.O. Box 341445
Los Angeles, California 90034, USA
Telephone: 1-800-927-4152 (inside USA);
1-310-837-5283 (outside USA)
e-mail: bbt.usa@krishna.com
web: www.krishna.com

The Bhaktivedanta Book Trust
P.O. Box 380,
Riverstone, NSW 2765, Australia
Phone: +61-2-96276306 • Fax: +61-2-96276052
E-mail: bbt.wp@krishna.com

Text
Mukunda Goswami, Bhūtātmā Dāsa (Austin Gordon), Drutakarmā Dāsa (Michael A. Cremo), and Mahārudra Dāsa (Jeff Long)

Art
Cover painting: Śrīnivāsa Dāsa
Black-and-white drawings: Locana Dāsa, Śrīnivāsa Dāsa
Color art: Parīkṣit Dāsa, Bharadrāja Dāsa, Dhṛti Dāsī

Previous printings: 2,730,000
Current printing, 2015: 50,000

Printed in China

ISBN 0-89213-114-4

DEDICATION

We dedicate this book to our beloved spiritual master and guide, His Divine Grace A. C. Bhaktivedanta Swami Prabhupāda, who brought the transcendental teachings of Lord Kṛṣṇa, including the authorized science of reincarnation, to the Western World.

BOOKS by His Divine Grace
A. C. Bhaktivedanta Swami Prabhupāda

Bhagavad-gītā As It Is
Śrīmad-Bhāgavatam (completed by disciples)
Śrī Caitanya-caritāmṛta
Kṛṣṇa, the Supreme Personality of Godhead
Teachings of Lord Caitanya
The Nectar of Devotion
The Nectar of Instruction
Śrī Īśopaniṣad
Light of the Bhāgavata
Easy Journey to Other Planets
Teachings of Lord Kapila, the Son of Devahūti
Teachings of Queen Kuntī
Message of Godhead
The Science of Self-Realization
The Perfection of Yoga
Beyond Birth and Death
On the Way to Kṛṣṇa
Rāja-vidyā: The King of Knowledge
Elevation to Kṛṣṇa Consciousness
Kṛṣṇa Consciousness: The Matchless Gift
Kṛṣṇa Consciousness: The Topmost Yoga System
Perfect Questions, Perfect Answers
Life Comes from Life
The Nārada-bhakti-sūtra (completed by disciples)
The Mukunda-mālā-stotra (completed by disciples)
Geetār-gān (Bengali)
Vairāgya-vidyā (Bengali)
Buddhi-yoga (Bengali)
Bhakti-ratna-boli (Bengali)
Back to Godhead magazine (founder)

BOOKS compiled from the teachings of His Divine Grace
A. C. Bhaktivedanta Swami Prabhupāda after his lifetime

Search for Liberation
Bhakti-yoga, the Art of Eternal Love
The Journey of Self-Discovery
Dharma, the Way of Transcendence
The Hare Kṛṣṇa Challenge
Renunciation Through Wisdom
A Second Chance
Beyond Illusion and Doubt
Civilization and Transcendence
Spiritual Yoga
The Laws of Nature
The Quest for Enlightenment

Contents

Preface

The Quest for Immortality

We were behaving like we were going to live forever, which is what everyone thought in the Beatles days, right? I mean, who-ever thought we were going to die?

—Beatle Paul McCartney

If you want to gain real control over your destiny, you must understand reincarnation and how it works. It's that simple.

No one wants to die. Most of us would like to live forever in full vigor, without wrinkles, gray hair, or arthritis. This is natural, because the first and most basic principle of life is to enjoy. If we could only enjoy life forever!

Man's eternal quest for immortality is so fundamental that we find it nearly impossible to conceive of dying. Pulitzer Prize winner William Saroyan (author of *The Human Comedy*) echoed the views of most people when, in the days just prior to his death, he announced to the media, "Everybody has got to die, but I have always believed an exception would be made in my case. Now what?"

Most of us seldom, if ever, think about death or what happens afterward. Some say that death is the end of everything. Some believe in heaven and hell. Still others hold that this life is only one of many we have lived and will live in the future. And more than one third of the world's population—over 2.5 billion people—accept reincarnation as an irrevocable fact of life.

Reincarnation is not a "belief system" or a psychological device for escaping the "grim finality" of death, but a precise science that explains our past and future lives. Many books have been written on the subject, usually based on hypnotic regression, near-death experiences, accounts of out-of-body experiences, or *deja-vu.*

But most reincarnation literature is poorly informed, highly speculative, superficial, and inconclusive. Some books purport to document cases of people who, under hypnosis, have been regressed to previous lifetimes. They describe in detail houses they lived in, streets they walked on, parks they frequented as children, and the names of their former parents, friends, and relatives. All this makes for interesting reading, and while such books have certainly stimulated the ever widening public interest and belief in reincarnation, careful investigations have revealed that many of these so-called past-life regression cases are rife with guesswork, inaccuracies, and even fraud.

But most importantly, none of these popular works explain the fundamental facts about reincarnation, like the simple process by which the soul perpetually transmigrates from one material body to another. In the rare instances when basic principles are discussed, authors generally present their own theories about how and in which particular cases reincarnation occurs, as if some special or gifted living beings reincarnate and others do not. This type of presentation does not deal with the science of reincarnation but introduces, instead, a confusing array of fabrications and contradictions, leaving the reader with scores of unanswered questions.

For example: Does one reincarnate instantaneously or slowly, over a long period of time? Can other living beings, like animals, reincarnate in human bodies? Can man appear as an animal? If so, how and why? Do we reincarnate forever, or does it end somewhere? Can the soul suffer eternally in hell or enjoy forever in heaven? Can we control our future incarnations? How? Can we be reborn on other planets or in other universes? Do good and evil actions play a role in determining our next body? What is the relationship between karma and reincarnation?

Coming Back fully answers these questions, because it scientifically explains the true nature of reincarnation. Finally, this book provides the reader with practical instructions on how to come to grips with and rise above the mysterious and generally misunderstood phenomenon of reincarnation-a reality that plays a vital role in shaping man's destiny.

"In my search for the secret of life, I ended up with atoms and electrons, which have no life at all. Somewhere along the line, life has run out through my fingers." —Nobel laureate Albert Szent-Györgi. *(p. xv)*

Introduction

The Mystery of Consciousness

Death. Man's most mysterious, relentless, and inevitable adversary. Does death mean the end of life, or does it merely open the door to another life, another dimension, or another world?

If man's consciousness survives the death experience, then what determines its transition to new realities?

In order to gain a clear understanding of these mysteries, man has traditionally turned to enlightened philosophers, accepting their teachings as representative of a higher truth.

Some criticize this method of acquiring knowledge from a higher authority, no matter how carefully the seeker may analyze it. Social philosopher E. F. Schumacher, author of *Small Is Beautiful*, notes that in our modern society, when people are out of touch with nature and traditional wisdom, they "consider it fashionable to ridicule . . . and only believe in what they see and touch and measure." Or, as the saying goes, "Seeing is believing."

But when man endeavors to understand something beyond the scope of the material senses, beyond instruments of measurement and the faculty of mental speculation, then there is no alternative but to approach a higher source of knowledge.

No scientist has successfully explained through laboratory investigations the mystery of consciousness or its destination after the destruction of the material body. Research in this field has produced many divergent theories, but their limitations must be recognized.

The systematic principles of reincarnation, on the other hand, comprehensively explain the subtle laws governing our past, present, and future lives.

If we are to understand reincarnation at all, we must acknowledge the fundamental concept of consciousness as an energy distinct from and superior to the matter composing the physical body. This principle is supported by examination of the unique thinking, feeling, and willing capacities of the human being. Can DNA strands or other genetic components possibly induce the feelings of love and respect one person has for another? What atom or molecule is responsible for the subtle artistic nuances in Shakespeare's *Hamlet or* Bach's "Mass in B Minor"? Man and his infinite capabilities cannot be explained by mere atoms and molecules. Einstein, the father of modern physics, admitted that consciousness could not be adequately described in terms of physical phenomena. "I believe that the present fashion of applying the axioms of science to human life is not only entirely a mistake but also has something reprehensible in it," the great scientist once said.

Indeed, scientists have failed to explain consciousness by means of the physical laws that govern everything else within their purview. Frustrated by this failing, Albert Szent-Györgyi, a Nobel laureate in physiology and medicine, once lamented, "In my search for the secret of life, I ended up with atoms and electrons, which have no life at all. Somewhere along the line, life has run out through my fingers. So, in my old age, I am now retracing my steps."

Accepting the notion that consciousness arises from molecular interaction requires an enormous leap of faith, much greater than that required for a metaphysical explanation. As Thomas Huxley, a leading biologist of his day and a contemporary of Charles Darwin, said, "It seems to me pretty plain that there is a third thing in the universe, to wit, consciousness, which . . . I cannot see to be matter or force or any conceivable modification of either."

Further recognition of the unique properties of consciousness was given by Nobel laureate in physic Niels Bohr, who remarked, "We can admittedly find nothing in physics or chemistry that has even a remote bearing on consciousness. Yet all of us know there is such a thing as consciousness, simply because we have it ourselves. Hence consciousness must be part of nature, or, more generally, of reality, which means that quite apart from the laws of physics and chemistry, as laid down in quantum theory, we must also consider laws of quite a different kind." Such laws might well include the laws of reincarnation, which govern the passage of consciousness from one physical body into another.

To begin understanding these laws, we may note that reincarnation is not an alien, antipodal event, but one that occurs with regularity in our own bodies during this very lifetime. In *The Human Brain,* Professor John Pfeiffer notes, "Your body does not contain a single one of the molecules that it contained seven years ago." Every seven years one's old body is completely rejuvenated. The self, however, our real identity, remains unchanged. Our bodies grow from infancy, to youth, to middle age, and then to old age, yet the person within the body, the "I,"always remains the same.

Reincarnation-based on the principle of a conscious self independent of its physical body-is part of a higher-order system governing the living being's transmigration from one material form to another. Since reincarnation deals with our most essential selves, it is a subject of the utmost relevance to everyone.

Coming Back explains the fundamentals of reincarnation presented in the timeless Vedic text *Bhagavad-gītā*. The *Gītā,* thousands of years older than the Dead Sea Scrolls, provides the most complete explanation of reincarnation available anywhere. It has been studied for millennia by many of the world's greatest thinkers, and since spiritual knowledge is eternally true and does not change with each new scientific theory, it is still relevant today.

Harvard biophysicist D. P. Dupey writes, "We may lead ourselves down a blind alley by adhering dogmatically to the assumption that life can be explained entirely by what we know of the laws of nature. By remaining open to the ideas embodied in the Vedic tradition of India, modern scientists can see their own disciplines from a new perspective and further the aim of all scientific endeavor: the search for truth."

In this age of global uncertainty, it is imperative that we understand the real origin of our conscious selves, how we find ourselves in different bodies and conditions of life, and what our destinations will be at the time of death. This essential information is comprehensively explained in *Coming Back.*

Chapter one shows how reincarnation has profoundly influenced many of the world's greatest philosophers, writers, and artists, from Socrates to Salinger. Next, the process of reincarnation as expounded in the *Bhagavad-gītā,* the oldest and most respected source book on the subject of transmigration of the soul, is presented.

Chapter two, a lively dialogue between His Divine Grace A.C. Bhaktivedanta Swami Prabhupāda and noted religious psychologist Karlfried Graf von Dürckheim, clearly shows how the material body and the antimaterial particle, the spirit soul, can never be the same. In chapter three a famous heart surgeon urges systematic research into the soul, and Śrīla Prabhupāda cites the Vedic version, thousands of years older and strikingly more informative than modern medical science. Three fascinating narratives from the Vedic text *Śrīmad-Bhāgavatam* constitute chapter four. These accounts stand as classic examples of how the soul transmigrates through different types of bodies under the control of the precise laws of nature and *karma*.

In chapter five, excerpts from the writings of Śrīla Prabhupāda clearly demonstrate that the principles of reincarnation can be easily understood in terms of ordinary events and common observations that regularly occur in our daily lives. The next chapter describes how reincarnation embodies a universal and infallible system of justice, wherein the soul is never banished to eternal damnation but is constitutionally endowed with a permanent opportunity to escape the perpetual cycle of birth and death.

Common misconceptions and chic notions about reincarnation form the subject of chapter seven, and the concluding chapter, "Don't Come Back," presents the process through which the soul can transcend reincarnation and enter realms in which it is finally freed from the prison of the material body. Having once achieved this status, the soul never again returns to this endlessly mutable world of birth, disease, old age, and death.

"Finding myself to exist in the world, I believe I shall, in some shape or other, always exist." —Benjamin Franklin. (*p.* 6)

1

Reincarnation: Socrates to Salinger

For the soul there is neither birth nor death at any time. He has not come into being, does not come into being, and will not come into being. He is unborn, eternal, ever-existing, and primeval. He is not slain when the body is slain.

—*Bhagavad-gītā* 2.20

Does life begin with birth and end with death? Have we lived before? Such questions are normally identified with religions of the East, where the life of man is known to endure not only from the cradle to the grave but through millions of ages, and acceptance of the idea of rebirth is nearly universal. As Arthur Schopenhauer, the great nineteenth-century German philosopher, once observed, "Were an Asiatic to ask me for a definition of Europe, I should be forced to answer him: It is that part of the world which is haunted by the incredible delusion that man was created out of nothing, and that his present birth is his first entrance into life."[1]

Indeed, the dominant ideology of the West, material science, has for several centuries stifled any serious or widespread interest in the preexistence and survival of consciousness beyond the present body. But throughout Western history there have always been thinkers who have understood and affirmed the immortality of consciousness and transmigration of the soul. And a multitude of philosophers, authors, artists, scientists, and politicians have given the idea thoughtful consideration.

Ancient Greece

Among the ancient Greeks, Socrates, Pythagoras, and Plato may be numbered among those who made reincarnation an integral part of their teachings. At the end of his life Socrates said, "I am confident that there truly is such a thing as living again, and that the living spring from the dead."[2] Pythagoras claimed he could remember his past lives, and Plato presented detailed accounts of reincarnation in his major works. Briefly, he held that the pure soul falls from the plane of absolute reality because of sensual desire and then takes on a physical body. The fallen souls first take birth in human forms, the highest of which is that of the philosopher, who strives for higher knowledge. If his knowledge becomes perfect, the philosopher can return to an eternal existence. But if he becomes hopelessly entangled in material desires, he descends into the animal species of life. Plato believed that gluttons and drunkards may become asses in future lives, violent and unjust people may take birth as wolves and hawks, and blind followers of social convention may become bees or ants. After some time, the soul again attains the human form and another chance to achieve liberation.[3] Some scholars believe that Plato and other early Greek philosophers derived their knowledge of reincarnation from mystery religions like Orphism, or from India.

Judaism, Christianity, Islam

Hints of reincarnation are also common in the history of Judaism and early Christianity. Information about past and future lives is found throughout the Cabala, which according to many Hebraic scholars represents the hidden wisdom behind the scriptures. In the Zohar, one of the principal Cabalistic texts, it is said, "The souls must reenter the absolute substance whence they have emerged. But to accomplish this, they must develop all the perfections, the germ of which is planted in them; and if they have not fulfilled this condition during one life, they must commence another, a third, and so forth, until they have acquired the condition which fits them for reunion with God."[4] According to the *Universal Jewish Encyclopedia,* Hasidic Jews hold similar beliefs.[5]

In the third century A.D., the theologian Origen, one of the fathers of the early Christian Church and its most accomplished Biblical scholar, wrote, "By some inclination toward evil, certain souls . . . come into bodies, first of men; then through their association with the irrational passions, after the allotted span of human life, they are changed into beasts, from which they sink to the level of . . . plants. From this condition they rise again through the same stages and are restored to their heavenly place."[6]

There are many passages in the Bible itself indicating that Christ and his followers were aware of the principle of reincarnation. Once, the disciples of Jesus asked him about the Old Testament prophecy that Elias would reappear on earth. In the Gospel of St. Matthew we read, "And Jesus answered them, Elias shall truly first come and restore all things. But I say unto you that Elias is come already and they knew him not. . . . Then the disciples understood that he spake unto them of John the Baptist."[7] In other words, Jesus declared that John the Baptist was a reincarnation of the prophet Elias. In another instance Jesus and his disciples came across a man blind from birth. The disciples asked Jesus, "Who sinned, this man or his parents, that he was born blind?"[8] Regardless who had sinned, Jesus replied, here was a chance to show a work of God. He then cured the man. Now, had the man been born blind for a sin of his own, it must have been a sin done before his birth—that is, in a previous life. And this was a suggestion that Jesus did not dispute.

The Koran says, "And you were dead, and He brought you back to life. And He shall cause you to die, and shall bring you back to life, and in the end shall gather you unto Himself."[9] Among the followers of Islam, the Sufis especially believe that death is no loss because the immortal soul continually passes through different bodies. Jalalu 'D-Din Rumi, a famous Sufi poet, writes,

I died as a mineral and became a plant,
I died as a plant and rose to animal,
I died as animal and I was man.
Why should I fear? When was I less by dying?[10]

The timeless Vedic scriptures of India confirm that the soul, according to its identification with material nature, takes one of 8,400,000 forms and, once embodied in a certain species of life, evolves automatically from lower to higher forms, ultimately attaining a human body.

Thus all the major Western religions—Judaism, Christianity, and Islam—have definite threads of reincarnation throughout the fabric of their teachings, even though the official custodians of dogma ignore or deny them.

The Middle Ages and the Renaissance

Under circumstances that to this day remain shrouded in mystery, in 553 A.D. the Byzantine emperor Justinian banned the teachings of preexistence of the soul from the Roman Catholic Church. During that era, numerous Church writings were destroyed, and many scholars now believe that references to reincarnation were purged from the scriptures. The Gnostic sects, however, although severely persecuted by the church, did manage to keep alive the doctrine of reincarnation in the West. (The word *gnostic* is derived from the Greek *gnosis,* meaning "knowledge.")

During the European Renaissance (spanning roughly the 14th through the 17th centuries) a new flowering of public interest in reincarnation occurred. One of the prominent figures in the revival was Italy's leading philosopher and poet, Giordano Bruno, whom the Inquisition ultimately sentenced to be burned at the stake because of his teachings about reincarnation. In his final answers to the charges brought against him, Bruno defiantly proclaimed that the soul "is not the body" and that "it may be in one body or in another, and pass from body to body."[11]

Because of such suppression by the Church, the teachings of reincarnation then went deeply underground, surviving in Europe in the secret societies of the Rosicrucians, Freemasons, Cabalists, and others.

The Age of Enlightenment

During the Age of Enlightenment (roughly the eighteenth century), European intellectuals began to free themselves from the constraints of Church censorship. The great philosopher Voltaire wrote that the doctrine of reincarnation is "neither absurd nor useless," adding, "It is not more surprising to be born twice than once."[12]

One may be surprised to note that several of America's founding fathers were fascinated by and ultimately accepted the idea of reincarnation, as interest in the subject made its way across the Atlantic to America. Expressing his firm belief, Benjamin Franklin wrote, "finding myself to exist in the world, I believe I shall, in some shape or other, always exist."[13]

In 1814 former U.S. President John Adams, who had been reading books about the Hindu religion, wrote another ex-president, Thomas Jefferson ("the sage of Monticello"), about the doctrine of reincarnation. After revolting against the Supreme Being, Adams wrote, some souls were hurled "down to the regions of total darkness. . . . [They were then] released from prison, permitted to ascend to earth and migrate into all sorts of animals, reptiles, birds, beasts, and men, according to their rank and character, and even into vegetables and minerals, there to serve on probation. If they passed without reproach their several graduations, they were permitted to become cows and men. If as men they behaved well . . . they were restored to their original rank and bliss in Heaven."[14]

In Europe, Napoleon was fond of telling his generals that in a previous life he was Charlemagne.[15] Johann Wolfgang von Goethe, one of the greatest German writers, also believed in reincarnation and may have encountered the idea in his readings in Indian philosophy. Goethe, renowned as a scientist as well, once remarked, "I am certain that I have been here as I am now a thousand times before, and I hope to return a thousand times."[16]

Transcendentalism

Interest in reincarnation and Indian philosophy also ran strong among the American Transcendentalists, including Emerson, Whitman, and Thoreau. Emerson wrote, "It is a secret of the world that all things subsist and do not die, but only retire a little from sight and afterwards return again. . . . Nothing is dead; men feign themselves dead and endure mock funerals and mournful obituaries, and there they stand looking out of the window, sound and well, in some new and strange disguise."[17] From the *Kaṭha Upaniṣad*, one of the many books of ancient Indian philosophy in his library, Emerson quoted: "The soul is not born; it does not die; it was not produced from anyone. . . . Unborn, eternal, it is not slain though the body is slain."[18]

Thoreau, the philosopher of Walden Pond, wrote, "As far back as I can remember, I have unconsciously referred to the experiences of a previous state of existence."[19] Another sign of Thoreau's deep interest in reincarnation is a manuscript, discovered in 1926, entitled "The Transmigration of the Seven Brahmanas." This short work is an English translation of a story about reincarnation from an ancient Sanskrit history. The transmigration episode follows the lives of seven sages through progressive incarnations as hunters, princes, and animals.

And Walt Whitman, in his poem "Song of Myself," writes,

> I know I am deathless . . .
> We have thus far exhausted
>   trillions of winters and summers,
> There are trillions ahead, and
>   trillions ahead of them.[20]

In France, famed author Honore Balzac wrote an entire novel about reincarnation, *Seraphita.* There Balzac states, "All human beings go through a previous life. . . . Who knows how many fleshly forms the heir of heaven occupies before he can be brought to understand the value of that silence and solitude whose starry plains are but the vestibule of spiritual worlds?"[21]

In *David Copperfield,* Charles Dickens explores an experience that hints at remembrances from past lives, *deja-vu.* "We all have some experience of a feeling that comes over us occasionally, of what we are saying and doing having been said and done before in a remote time—of our having been surrounded, dim ages ago, by the same faces, objects, and circumstances.[22]

And in Russia, the eminent Count Leo Tolstoy wrote, "As we live through thousands of dreams in our present life, so is our present life only one of many thousands of such lives which we enter from the other, more real life . . . and then return after death. Our life is but one of the dreams of that more real life, and so it is endlessly, until the very last one, the very real life—the life of God."[23]

The Modern Age

As we enter the twentieth century, we find the idea of reincarnation attracting the mind of one of the West's most influential artists, Paul Gauguin, who during his final years in Tahiti wrote that when the physical organism breaks down "the soul survives." It then takes on another body, Gauguin wrote, "degrading or elevating according to merit or demerit." The artist believed that the idea of continual rebirth had first been taught in the West by Pythagoras, who had learned it from the sages of ancient India.[24]

U. S. auto magnate Henry Ford once told a newspaper interviewer, "I adopted the theory of reincarnation when I was twenty-six." Ford said, "Genius is experience. Some seem to think that it is a gift or talent, but it is the fruit of long experience in many lives."[25] In a similar fashion, General George S. Patton believed he had acquired his military skills on ancient battlefields.

Reincarnation is a recurring theme in James Joyce's *Ulysses*. In one passage Joyce's hero, Leopold Bloom, tells his wife, "Some people believe we go on living in another body after death, that we lived before. They call it reincarnation. That we all lived before on the earth thousands of years ago or on some other planet. They say we have forgotten it. Some say they remember their past lives."[26]

Jack London made reincarnation the major theme of his novel *The Star Rover,* in which the central character says, "I did not begin when I was born, nor when I was conceived. I have been growing, developing through incalculable myriads of millenniums. . . . All my previous selves have their voices, echoes, promptings in me. . . . Oh, incalculable times again shall I be born, and yet the stupid dolts about me think that by stretching my neck with a rope they will make me cease."[27]

Nobel laureate Herman Hesse wrote the following in his classic novel about the search for spiritual truth, *Siddhartha:* "He saw all these forms and faces in a thousand relationships to each other. . . . None of them died, they only changed, were always reborn, continually had a new face: only time stood between one face and another."[28]

Numerous scientists and psychologists have believed in reincarnation as well. One of the most influential psychologists, Carl Jung, used the concept of an eternal self that undergoes many births as a tool in his attempts to understand the deepest mysteries of the self and consciousness. "I could well imagine that I might have lived in former centuries and there encountered questions I was not yet able to answer; that I had to be born again because I had not fulfilled the task that was given to me,"[29] Jung wrote.

British biologist Thomas Huxley noted that "the doctrine of transmigration" was a "means of constructing a plausible vindication of the ways of the cosmos to man," and warned that "none but very hasty thinkers will reject it on the grounds of inherent absurdity."[30]

One of the leading figures in the field of psychoanalysis and human development, American psychoanalyst Erik Erikson, who coined the phrase "identity crisis," was convinced that reincarnation goes to the very core of every man's belief system. "Let us face it: 'deep down' nobody in his right mind can visualize his own existence without assuming that he has always lived and will live hereafter,"[31] the author wrote.

Mahatma Gandhi, one of the greatest political figures of modern times and the apostle of nonviolence, once explained how a practical understanding of reincarnation gave him hope for his dream of world peace. Gandhi said, "I cannot think of permanent enmity between man and man, and believing as I do in the theory of rebirth, I live in the hope that if not in this birth, in some other birth I shall be able to hug all of humanity in friendly embrace."[32]

J. D. Salinger, in one of his most famous short stories, "Teddy," introduces a precocious young boy of that name who recalls his reincarnation experiences and speaks forthrightly about them. "It's so silly. All you do is get the heck out of your body when you die. My gosh, everybody's done it thousands of times. Just because they don't remember, it doesn't mean they haven't done it."[33]

Jonathan Livingston Seagull, the eponymous hero of the novel by Richard Bach, is described there as "that brilliant little fire that burns within us all." He goes through a series of reincarnations that lead him from earth to a heavenly world and back again, to enlighten the less fortunate gulls. One of Jonathan's mentors inquires, "Do you have any idea how many lives we must have gone through before we even got the first idea that there is more to life than eating, or fighting, or power in the Flock? A thousand lives, Jon, ten thousand! And then another hundred lives until we began to learn that there is such a thing as perfection, and another hundred again to get the idea that our purpose for living is to find that perfection and show it forth."[34]

Nobel laureate Isaac Bashevis Singer, in his masterful short stories, often spoke of past lives, rebirth, and the immortality of the soul. "There is no death. How can there be death if everything is part of the Godhead? The soul never dies and the body is never really alive."[35]

And British poet laureate John Masefield, in his well-known poem about past and future lives, writes,

> I hold that when a person dies
> His soul returns again to earth;
> Arrayed in some new flesh disguise
> Another mother gives him birth
> With sturdier limbs and brighter brain
> The old soul takes the road again.[36]

Musician, songwriter, and celebrated Beatle George Harrison thought seriously about reincarnation, as revealed in his private thoughts on interpersonal relationships. "Friends are all souls that we've known in other lives. We're drawn to each other. That's how I feel about friends. Even if I have only known them a day, it doesn't matter. I'm not going to wait till I have known them for two years, because anyway, we must have met somewhere before, you know."[37]

For some time reincarnation has been attracting the minds of intellectuals and the general public in the West. Films, novels, popular songs, and periodicals now treat reincarnation with ever-increasing frequency, and millions of Westerners are rapidly joining ranks with the more than two billion people, including Hindus, Buddhists, Taoists, and members of other faiths, who have traditionally understood that life does not begin at birth or end at death. But simple curiosity or belief is not sufficient. It is merely the first step in understanding the complete science of reincarnation, which includes knowledge of how to free oneself from the miserable cycle of birth and death.

The Bhagavad-gītā: The Timeless Sourcebook on Reincarnation

Many Westerners, in order to gain a deeper understanding about reincarnation, are turning to the original sources of knowledge about past and future lives. Among all available literatures, the Sanskrit *Vedas* of India are the oldest on earth and present the most comprehensive and logical explanations of the science of reincarnation, teachings that have maintained their viability and universal appeal for more than five thousand years.

The most fundamental information about reincarnation appears in the *Bhagavad-gītā,* the essence of the *Upaniṣads* and of all Vedic knowledge. The *Gītā* was spoken fifty centuries ago by Lord Kṛṣṇa, the Supreme Personality of Godhead, to His friend and disciple Arjuna on a battlefield in northern India. A battlefield is the perfect place for a discussion about reincarnation, for in combat men directly confront the fateful questions of life, death, and the afterlife.

As Kṛṣṇa begins to speak on the immortality of the soul, He tells Arjuna, "Never was there a time when I did not exist, nor you, nor all these kings; nor in the future shall any of us cease to be."[38] The *Gītā* further instructs, "That which pervades the entire body you should know to be indestructible. No one is able to destroy that imperishable soul."[39] The soul—here we speak of something so subtle that it is not immediately verifiable by the limited human mind and senses. Therefore, not everyone will be able to accept the existence of the soul. Kṛṣṇa informs Arjuna, "Some look on the soul as amazing, some describe him as amazing, and some hear of him as amazing, while others, even after hearing about him, cannot understand him at all."[40]

On the Battlefield of Kurukṣetra, Lord Kṛṣṇa instructs his friend and devotee Arjuna about the science of reincarnation.

Accepting the existence of the soul is, however, not merely a matter of faith. The *Bhagavad-gītā* appeals to the evidence of our senses and to logic so that we may accept its teachings with some degree of rational conviction and not blindly, as dogma.

It is impossible to understand reincarnation unless one knows the difference between the actual self (the soul) and the body. The *Gītā* helps us see the nature of the soul by the following example. "As the sun alone illuminates all this universe, so does the living entity, one within the body, illuminate the entire body by consciousness."[41]

Consciousness is concrete evidence of the presence of the soul within the body. On an overcast day the sun is not visible, but we know it is there in the sky by the presence of sunlight. Similarly, at present we cannot directly perceive the soul in the body, but we may conclude it is there by the presence of consciousness. In the absence of consciousness, the body is simply a lump of dead matter. Only the presence of consciousness makes this lump of dead matter breathe, speak, love, and fear. In essence, the body is a vehicle for the soul, through which it may fulfill its myriad material desires. The *Gītā* explains that the living entity within the body is "seated as on a machine made of the material energy."[42] The soul falsely identifies with the body, carrying its different conceptions of life from one body to another as the air carries aromas. Just as an automobile cannot function without the presence of a driver, similarly, the material body cannot function without the presence of the soul.

As one grows older, this distinction between the conscious self and the physical body becomes more obvious. Within his lifetime a person can observe that his body is constantly changing. It does not endure, and time proves the child ephemeral. The body comes into existence at a certain time, grows, matures, produces by-products (children), and gradually dwindles and dies. The physical body is thus unreal, for it will, in due time, disappear. As the *Gītā* explains, "Of the nonexistent there is no endurance."[43] But despite all the changes of the material body, consciousness, a symptom of the soul within, remains unchanged. ("Of the eternal there is no change."[44]) Therefore, we may logically conclude that consciousness possesses an innate quality of permanence that enables it to survive the dissolution of the body. Kṛṣṇa tells Arjuna, "For the soul there is neither birth nor death at any time. . . . He is not slain when the body is slain."[45]

But if the soul is "not slain when the body is slain," then what becomes of it? The answer given in the *Bhagavad-gītā* is that the soul enters another body. This is reincarnation. This concept may be difficult for some people to accept, but it is a natural phenomenon, and the *Gītā* gives logical examples to aid our understanding: "As the embodied soul continuously passes, in this body, from childhood to youth to old age, the soul similarly passes into another body at death. A sober person is not bewildered by such a change."[46]

In other words, the soul reincarnates even in the course of one lifetime. Any biologist will tell you that the body's cells are constantly dying and being replaced by new ones. In other words, each of us has a number of "different" bodies in this very life. The body of an adult is completely different from the body the same person had as an infant. Yet despite bodily changes, the person within remains the same. Something similar happens at the time of death. The self undergoes a final change of body. The *Gītā* says, "As a person puts on new garments, giving up old ones, the soul similarly accepts new material bodies, giving up the old and useless ones."[47] Thus the soul remains entrapped in an endless cycle of births and deaths. "One who has taken his birth is sure to die, and after death one is sure to take birth again,"[48] the Lord tells Arjuna.

According to the *Vedas,* there are 8,400,000 species of life, beginning with the microbes, rising through the fish, plants, insects, reptiles, birds, and animals to the humans and demigods. According to their desires, the living entities perpetually take birth in these species.

The mind is the mechanism that directs these transmigrations, propelling the soul to newer and newer bodies. The *Gītā* explains, "Whatever state of being one remembers when he quits his body, . . . that state he will attain without fail [in his next life]."[49] Everything we have thought and done during our life makes an impression on the mind, and the sum total of all these impressions influences our final thoughts at death. According to the quality of these thoughts, material nature awards us a suitable body. Therefore, the type of body that we have now is the expression of our consciousness at the time of our last death.

The *Gītā* explains: "The living entity, thus taking another gross body, obtains a certain type of ear, eye, tongue, nose, and sense of touch, which are grouped about the mind. He thus enjoys a particular set of sense objects."[50] Further, the path of reincarnation does not always lead upward, nor is a human being guaranteed a human birth in his next life. For example, if one dies with the mentality of a dog, then in his next life he will receive the eyes, ears, nose, etc., of a dog and be able to enjoy canine pleasures. Lord Kṛṣṇa confirms the fate of such an unfortunate soul, saying, "When one dies in the mode of ignorance, he takes birth in the animal kingdom."[51]

According to the *Bhagavad-gītā,* humans who do not inquire about their nonphysical, higher nature are compelled by the laws of karma to continue in the cycle of birth, death, and rebirth, sometimes appearing as humans, sometimes as animals, and sometimes as plants or insects.

Our existence in the material world is due to the multiple karmic reactions of this and previous lives, and the human body provides the only loophole through which the materially conditioned soul can escape. By properly utilizing the human form, one can solve all the problems of life (birth, death, disease, and old age) and break the endless cycle of reincarnation. If, however, a soul who has evolved to the human platform wastes his life by engaging only in activities for sense pleasure, he can easily create sufficient karma in this present life to keep him entangled in the cycle of birth and death for thousands upon thousands of lives. And they may not all be human.

Lord Kṛṣṇa says, "The foolish cannot understand how a living entity can quit his body, nor can they understand what sort of body he enjoys under the spell of the modes of nature. But one whose eyes are trained in knowledge can see all this. The endeavoring transcendentalists who are situated in self-realization can see all this clearly. But those whose minds are not developed and who are not situated in self-realization cannot see what is taking place, though they may try to."[52]

A soul fortunate enough to obtain a human body should seriously endeavor for self-realization, to understand the principles of reincarnation and become free from repeated birth and death. We can't afford not to.

Notes

1. *Parerga and Paralipomena,* II, Chapter 16.
2. *Phaedo,* translator Benjamin Jowett.
3. *Phaedrus.*
4. E. D. Walker, *Reincarnation: A Study of Forgotten Truth.* Boston: Houghton Miflin, 1888, p. 212.
5. Article, "Souls, Transmigration of."
6. *De Principiis,* Book III, Chapter 5. *Ante-Nicene Christian Library,* editors, Alexander Roberts and James Donaldson. Edinburgh: Clark, 1867.
7. Matthew 17:9–13.
8. John 9:2.
9. Sura 2:28.
10. R. A. Nicholson, *Rumi, Poet and Mystic.* London: Allen & Unwin, 1950, p. 103.
11. William Boulting, *Giordano Bruno: His Life, Thought, and Martyrdom,* London: Kegan Paul, 1914. pp. 163–64.
12. Quoted in Emil Block's *Widerholt Erdenleben.* Stuttgart: 1952, p. 31.
13. Letter to George Whatley, May 23, 1785. *The Works of Benjamin Franklin,* editor, Jared Sparks, Boston: 1856, X, p. 174.
14. Letter to Thomas Jefferson, March 1814. *Correspondence of John Adams.*
15. Emil Ludwig, *Napoleon.* NY: Boni & Liveright, 1926, p. 245.
16. *Memoirs of Johannes Falk.* Leipzig: 1832. Reprinted in *Goethe-Bibliothek,* Berlin: 1911.
17. *The Selected Writings of Ralph Waldo Emerson,* editor, Brooks Atkinson, New York: Modern Library, 1950, p. 445.
18. *Emerson's Complete Works.* Boston: Houghton Miflin, 1886, IV. p. 35.
19. *The Journal of Henry D. Thoreau.* Boston: Houghton Miflin, 1949, 11, p. 306.
20. *Walt Whitman's Leaves of Grass,* 1st (1855) edition, editor, Malcolm Cowley. New York: Viking, 1959.
21. *Balzac, La Comedie Humaine.* Boston: Pratt, 1904, XXXIX, pp. 175–76.
22. Chapter 39.
23. Moscow: Magazine, *The Voice of Universal Love,* 1908, No. 40, p. 634.

24. *Modern Thought and Catholicism,* translator, Frank Lester Pleadwell. Privately printed, 1927. The original manuscript is now held by the St. Louis Art Museum, St. Louis, Missouri.
25. *San Francisco Examiner,* August 28, 1928.
26. First episode, "Calypso."
27. New York: Macmillan, 1919, pp. 252–54.
28. New York: New Directions, 1951.
29. *Memories, Dreams, and Reflections.* New York: Pantheon, 1963, p. 323.
30. *Evolution and Ethics and Other Essays.* New York: Appleton, 1894, pp. 60–61.
31. *Gandhi's Truth.* New York: Norton, 1969, p. 36.
32. *Young India,* April 2, 1931, p. 54.
33. J. D. Salinger, *Nine Stories.* New York: Signet paperback, 1954.
34. New York: Macmillan, 1970, pp. 53–54.
35. A *Friend of Kafka and Other Stories.* New York: Farrar, Straus & Giroux, 1962.
36. "A Creed," *Collected Poems.*
37. *I, Me, Mine.* New York: Simon and Schuster, 1980.
38. *Bhagavad-gītā* 2.12
39. *Bhagavad-gītā* 2.17
40. *Bhagavad-gītā* 2.29
41. *Bhagavad-gītā* 13.34
42. *Bhagavad-gītā* 18.61
43. *Bhagavad-gītā* 2.16
44. *Bhagavad-gītā* 2.16
45. *Bhagavad-gītā* 2.20
46. *Bhagavad-gītā* 2.13
47. *Bhagavad-gītā* 2.22
48. *Bhagavad-gītā* 2.27
49. *Bhagavad-gītā* 8.6
50. *Bhagavad-gītā* 15.9
51. *Bhagavad-gītā* 14.15
52. *Bhagavad-gītā* 15.10–11

The body is really only a mental structure, somewhat like a dream, but the self is different from all of these mental structures. That is self-realization. (*p.* 27)

2

Changing Bodies

In 1974, at the ISKCON center in the countryside near Frankfurt, West Germany, His Divine Grace A. C. Bhaktivedanta Swami Prabhupāda had the following dialogue with Professor Karlfried Graf von Dürckheim. Professor Dürckheim, a noted religious psychologist and the author of The Way of Transformation: Daily Life as Spiritual Practice, *held a Ph.D. in analytic psychology and was renowned for establishing a therapeutic school in Bavaria that incorporated both Western and Eastern approaches to the psychology of consciousness. In this conversation Śrīla Prabhupāda explains the first and most basic principle of reincarnation—that the spiritual living entity is different from the material body. After establishing that the conscious self and the body are separate entities, Śrīla Prabhupāda describes how the conscious self, or soul, perpetually transmigrates to another body at the time of death.*

Professor Dürckheim: In my work, I've found that the natural ego doesn't like to die. But if you go through it [a near-death experience], you seem to cross the threshold of death to quite a different reality.

Śrīla Prabhupāda: Yes, it is different. The experience is like that of a diseased person regaining his health.

Prof. Dürckheim: So the person who is dead experiences a higher level of reality?

Śrīla Prabhupāda: It's not the person who has died, but the body. According to Vedic knowledge, the body is always dead. For example, a microphone is made of metal. When electric energy passes through the microphone, it responds by converting sound into electrical impulses, which are amplified and broadcast over loudspeakers. But when there is no electricity in the system, nothing happens. Whether the microphone is working or not, it remains nothing more than an assembly of metal, plastic, etc. Similarly, the human body works because of the living force within. When this living force leaves the body, it is said that the body is dead. But actually it is always dead. The living force is the important element; its presence alone makes the body appear to be alive. But "alive" or "dead," the physical body is nothing more than a collection of dead matter.

The first teaching of the *Bhagavad-gītā* reveals that the condition of the material body is ultimately not very important.

aśocyān anvaśocas tvaṁ
prajñā-vādāṁś ca bhāṣase
gatāsūn agatāsūṁś ca
nānuśocanti paṇḍitāḥ

"The Supreme Personality of Godhead said: While speaking learned words you are mourning for what is not worthy of grief. Those who are wise lament neither for the living nor the dead." [Bg. 2.11]

The dead body is not the real subject for philosophical inquiry. Rather, we should concern ourselves with the active principle—the principle that makes the dead body move—the soul.

Prof. Dürckheim: How do you teach your disciples to become aware of this force which is not matter but which makes matter appear alive? I can intellectually appreciate that you're speaking a philosophy which contains the truth. I don't doubt it. But how do you make a person feel it?

How to Perceive the Soul

Śrīla Prabhupāda: It's a very simple matter. There is an active principle which makes the body move; when it is absent, the body no longer moves. So the real question is, "What is that active principle?" This inquiry lies at the heart of Vedānta philosophy. In fact, the *Vedānta-sūtra* begins with the aphorism *athāto brahma-jijñāsā*—"What is the nature of the self within the body?" Therefore, the student of Vedic philosophy is first taught to distinguish the difference between a living body and a dead one. If he is unable to grasp this principle, we then ask him to consider the problem from the standpoint of logic. Anyone can see that the body is changing and moving because of the presence of the active principle, the soul. In the absence of the active principle, the body neither changes nor moves. So there must be something within the body that makes it move. It is not a very difficult concept.

The body is always dead. It is like a big machine. A tape recorder is made of dead matter, but as soon as you, the living person, push a button, it works. Similarly, the body is also dead matter. But within the body is the life force. As long as this active principle remains within the body, the body responds and appears alive. For instance, we all have the power to speak. If I ask one of my students to come here, he will come. But if the active principle leaves his body, I may call him for thousands of years, but he will not come. This is very simple to understand.

But what exactly is that active principle? That is a separate subject matter, and the answer to that question is the real beginning of spiritual knowledge.

Prof. Dürckheim: I can understand the point you made about the dead body—that there must be something within to make it alive. The only proper conclusion is that we are talking about two things—the body and the active principle. But my real question is, How do we become aware of the active principle within ourselves as a direct experience and not simply as an intellectual conclusion? On the inner path isn't it important to actually experience this deeper reality?

"I Am Brahman, Spirit"

Śrīla Prabhupāda: You yourself *are* that active principle. The living body and the dead body are different. The only difference is the presence of the active principle. When it is not there, the body is called dead. So the real self is identical with the active principle. In the *Vedas* we find the maxim *so 'ham*—"I am the active principle." It is also said, *ahaṁ brahmāsmi:* "I am not this material body. I am Brahman, spirit." That is self-realization. The self-realized person is described in the *Bhagavad-gītā. Brahma-bhūtaḥ prasannātmā na śocati na kāṅkṣati:* when one is self-realized, he neither hankers nor laments. *Samaḥ sarveṣu bhūteṣu:* he is equal to everyone—men, animals, all living beings.

Prof. Dürckheim: Consider this. One of your students might say, "I am spirit," but he might not be able to experience it.

Śrīla Prabhupāda: How can he *not* experience it? He knows that he is the active principle. Everyone ultimately knows that they are not the body. Even a child knows it. We can observe this by examining the way we speak. We say, "This is my finger." We never say, "I finger." So what is that "I"? This is self-realization—"I am not this body."

And this realization can be extended to other living

beings. Why does man kill animals? Why give trouble to others? One who is self-realized can see, "Here is another self. He simply has a different body, but the same active principle that exists within my body is operating within his body." The self-realized person sees all living entities with equal vision, knowing that the active principle, the self, is present not only in human beings but within the bodies of animals, birds, fish, insects, trees, and plants as well.

Reincarnation in This Life

The active principle is the soul, and the soul transmigrates from one body to another at the time of death. The body may be different, but the self remains the same. We can observe this change of body even within our own lifetime. We have transmigrated from babyhood to childhood, from childhood to youth, and from youth to adulthood. Yet all the while, the conscious self, or soul, has remained the same. The body is material, and the actual self is spiritual. When one comes to this understanding, he is called self-realized.

Prof. Dürckheim: I think we are now arriving at a very decisive moment in the Western world, because for the first time in our history people in Europe and America are starting to take seriously the inner experiences by which truth is revealed. Of course, in the East there have always been philosophers who have known the experiences by which death loses its terrifying character and becomes the threshold to a more complete life.

People need this experience of overcoming their usual bodily habits. And if they can break through that bodily experience, they suddenly realize that quite a different principle is operating within themselves. They become aware of the "inner life."

Śrīla Prabhupāda: A devotee of Lord Kṛṣṇa automatically realizes that different principle, because he never thinks,

"I am this body." He thinks, *ahaṁ brahmāsmi*—"I am spirit soul." The first instruction given by Lord Kṛṣṇa to Arjuna in the *Bhagavad-gītā* is this: "My dear Arjuna, you are very seriously considering the condition of the body, but a learned man does not take this material body, either dead or alive, very seriously." This is the first realization on the path of spiritual progress. Everyone in this world is very much concerned with the body, and when it is alive, they take care of it in so many ways. When it is dead, they erect grand statues and monuments over it. This is body consciousness. But no one understands that active principle which gives the body beauty and life. And at the time of death, no one knows where the real self, the active principle, has gone. That is ignorance.

Prof. Dürckheim: During World War I, when I was a young man, I spent four years at the front. I was one of two officers in my regiment who was not wounded. On the battlefield, I saw death again and again. I saw people standing just next to me get hit, and suddenly their life force was gone. All that was left, as you say, was a body without a soul. But when death was near and I accepted that I also might die, I realized that within myself was something that has nothing whatsoever to do with death.

Śrīla Prabhupāda: Yes. That is self-realization.

Prof. Dürckheim: This experience of war marked me very deeply. It was the beginning of my inner path.

Śrīla Prabhupāda: In the *Vedas* it is said, *nārāyaṇa-parāḥ sarve na kutaścana bibhyati.* If one is a God-realized soul, he is not afraid of anything.

Prof. Dürckheim: The process of self-realization is a sequence of inner experiences, isn't it? Here in Europe, the people have gone through such experiences. In fact, I believe this is the real treasure of Europe—that there are so many people who went through the battlefields, through the concentration camps, through the bombing raids. And within their hearts they retain the memories of those moments when death was near, when they were wounded and nearly torn to pieces, and they experienced a glimpse of their eternal nature. But now it's necessary to show people that they don't need a battlefield, a concentration camp, or a bombing raid in order to take seriously those inner experiences when one is suddenly touched by a sense of divine reality and understands that this bodily existence is not the all and all.

The Body Is Like a Dream

Śrīla Prabhupāda: We can experience that every night. When we dream, our body lies on the bed, but we go somewhere else. In this way we all experience that our real identity is separate from this body. When we dream we forget the body lying on the bed. We act in different bodies and in different locations. Similarly, during the day we forget our dream bodies in which we traveled to so many places. Perhaps in our dream bodies we flew in the sky. At night we forget our waking body, and in the daytime we forget our dream body. But our conscious self, the soul, still exists, and we remain aware of our existence in both bodies. Therefore, we must conclude that we are not any of these bodies. For some time we exist in a certain body, then at death we forget it. So the body is really only a mental structure, somewhat like a dream, but the self is different from all of these mental structures. That is self-realization. In the *Bhagavad-gītā* [3.42] Lord Kṛṣṇa says,

indriyāṇi parāṇy āhur
indriyebhyaḥ paraṁ manaḥ
manasas tu parā buddhir
yo buddheḥ paratas tu saḥ

"The working senses are superior to dull matter, mind is higher than the senses, intelligence is still higher than the mind, and he (the soul) is even higher than the intelligence."

Prof. Dürckheim: Earlier today you spoke about the false ego. Did you mean that the real ego is the soul?

Śrīla Prabhupāda: Yes, that is the pure ego. For instance, now I have this seventy-eight-year-old Indian body, and I have this false ego that thinks, "I am Indian," "I am this body." This is a misconception. Someday this temporary body will vanish and I'll get another temporary body. It's just a temporary illusion. The reality is that the soul, based on its desires and activities, transmigrates from one body to another.

Prof. Dürckheim: Can consciousness exist apart from the material body?

Śrīla Prabhupāda: Yes. Pure consciousness, the soul, does not need a material body. For instance, when you dream, you forget your present body, but you still remain conscious. The soul, the consciousness, is like water: water is pure, but as soon as it falls from the sky and touches the ground, it becomes muddy.

Prof. Dürckheim: Yes.

Śrīla Prabhupāda: Similarly, we are spirit souls, we are pure, but as soon as we leave the spiritual world and come in contact with these material bodies, our consciousness becomes covered. The consciousness remains pure, but now it is covered by mud (this body). And this is why people are fighting. They are wrongly identifying with the body, thinking, "I am German," "I am English," "I am American," "I am Indian," "I am black," "I am white," "I am this," "I am that"—so many bodily designations. These bodily designations are impurities. This is why artists sculpt or paint nude figures. In France, for example, they regard nakedness as "pure" art. Similarly, when you understand the "nakedness," or true condition, of the spirit

soul—without these bodily designations—that is purity.
Prof. Dürckheim: Why does it appear to be so difficult to understand that one is different from the body?

Everyone Knows "I Am Not This Body"

Śrīla Prabhupāda: It is *not* difficult. You *can* experience it. It is only because of foolishness that people think differently; but everyone really knows, "I am not this body." This is very easy to experience. I am existing. I understand that I have existed in a baby's body, I have existed in a child's body, and also in a boy's body. I have existed in so many bodies, and now I am in an old man's body. Or, for example, say you have now put on a black coat. The next moment you may put on a white coat. But you are not that black or white coat; you have simply changed coats. If I call you "Mr. Black Coat" or "Mr. White Coat," that is my foolishness. Similarly, in my lifetime I have changed bodies many times, but I am not any of these bodies. This is real knowledge.
Prof. Dürckheim: And yet isn't there a difficulty? For instance, you may have already intellectually understood very well that you are not the body—but you may still have the fear of death. Doesn't that mean you didn't understand it by experience? As soon as you've understood by experience, you should have no fear of death, because you know that you can't really die.
Śrīla Prabhupāda: Experience is received from a higher authority, from someone who has higher knowledge. Instead of my trying to experience for years and years that I am not this body, I can take the knowledge from God, or Kṛṣṇa, the perfect source. Then I have experienced my deathlessness by hearing from a bona fide authority. That is perfect.
Prof. Dürckheim: Yes, I understand.
Śrīla Prabhupāda: Therefore, the Vedic instruction is

tad-vijñānārthaṁ sa gurum evābhigacchet. "In order to get first-class experience of the perfection of life, you must approach a guru." And who is a guru? Whom should I approach? I should approach someone who has heard perfectly from his guru. This is called disciplic succession. I hear from a perfect person, and I distribute the knowledge in the same way, without any change. Lord Kṛṣṇa gives us knowledge in the *Bhagavad-gītā,* and we distribute the same knowledge, without changing it.

Prof. Dürckheim: Over the past twenty or thirty years there has been a great awakening of interest in spiritual topics in the Western part of the world. But, on the other hand, if the scientists want to eliminate the human self, they are well on the way to doing it with their atomic bombs and other technical innovations. If they want to guide humanity to some higher goal, however, then they have to stop looking at man in a materialistic way through their scientific spectacles. They must look at us as we are—conscious selves.

The Goal of Human Life

Śrīla Prabhupāda: The goal of human life is self-realization, or God realization, but the scientists do not know that. Modern society is presently led by blind and foolish men. The so-called technologists, scientists, and philosophers do not know the real aim of life. And the people themselves are blind as well; so we have a situation in which the blind are leading the blind. If a blind man tries to lead another blind man, what type of results can we expect? No; this is not the process. One must approach a self-realized person if he wants to understand the truth.

[*More guests enter the room.*]

Disciple: Śrīla Prabhupāda, these gentlemen are professors of theology and philosophy. And this is Doctor Dara. He

You have now put on a black coat. The next moment you may put on a white coat. But you are not that black or white coat. You have simply changed coats. (*p.* 29)

is the leader of a society for the study of yoga and integral philosophy here in Germany.

[*Śrīla Prabhupāda greets them and the conversation resumes.*]

Prof. Dürckheim: May I ask another question? Isn't there another level of experience that opens the door to some deeper consciousness for the common man?

Śrīla Prabhupāda: Yes. That experience is described by Kṛṣṇa in the *Bhagavad-gītā* [2.13]:

dehino 'smin yathā dehe
kaumāraṁ yauvanaṁ jarā
tathā dehāntara-prāptir
dhīras tatra na muhyati

"As the embodied soul continuously passes, in this body, from childhood to youth to old age, the soul similarly passes into another body at death. A sober person is not bewildered by such a change."

But first one must understand the basic principle of knowledge—that I am not this body. When one understands this basic principle, then he can advance to deeper knowledge.

Prof. Dürckheim: It seems to me that there is a big difference between the Eastern and Western approaches to this problem of body and soul. In the teachings of the East, you have to become free of the body, whereas in Western religions, a person tries to realize the spirit within the body.

Śrīla Prabhupāda: This is very easy to understand. We have heard from the *Bhagavad-gītā* that we are spirit, that we are within the body. Our sufferings come about because of our identification with the body. Because I have entered into this body, therefore I am suffering. So, either Eastern or Western, my real business should be how to get

out of this body. Is that point clear?
Prof. Dürckheim: Yes.
Śrīla Prabhupāda: The term *reincarnation* means that I am a spirit soul who has entered a body. But in my next life I will enter another body. It may be a dog's body, it may be a cat's body, or it may be a king's body. But there will be suffering—either in the king's body or in the dog's body. These sufferings include birth, death, old age, and disease. So in order to abolish these four kinds of suffering, we have to get out of the body. That is man's real problem—how to get out of his material body.
Prof. Dürckheim: This takes many lives?
Śrīla Prabhupāda: It can take many lives, or you can do it in one lifetime. If you understand in this life that your sufferings are due to this body, then you should inquire how to get out of the body. And when you get that knowledge, you will know the trick—how to get out of the body immediately.
Prof. Dürckheim: But that doesn't mean that I have to kill the body, does it? Doesn't it mean that I realize my spirit is independent from my body?
Śrīla Prabhupāda: No; it isn't necessary that the body be killed. But whether your body is killed or not, someday you will have to leave your present body and accept another one. That is nature's law, and you cannot avoid it.
Prof. Dürckheim: It seems that there are some points here which are in accordance with Christianity.
Śrīla Prabhupāda: It doesn't matter whether you are Christian, Muslim, or Hindu: knowledge is knowledge. Wherever knowledge is available, you must pick it up. And this is knowledge: every living being is imprisoned within a material body. This knowledge applies equally to Hindus, Muslims, Christians—everyone. The soul is imprisoned within the body and must therefore undergo birth, death,

old age, and disease. But we all want to live eternally, we want full knowledge, we want full blissfulness. To attain this goal we must get out of the body. This is the process.

Professor Dara: You stress the point that we must get out of the body. But shouldn't we accept our existence as human beings?

Śrīla Prabhupāda: You propose accepting our existence as human beings. Do you think that existing within this human body is perfect?

Prof. Dara: No, I don't say it is perfect. But we should accept this and not try to create some ideal situation.

How to Become Perfect

Śrīla Prabhupāda: You admit that your condition is not perfect. Therefore, the correct idea should be to discover how to become perfect.

Prof. Dara: But why do we have to become perfect as spirit? Why can't we become perfect as humans?

Śrīla Prabhupāda: You have already admitted that your situation within this human body is not perfect. So why are you so attached to this imperfect situation?

Prof. Dara: This body is an instrument through which I can communicate with other people.

Śrīla Prabhupāda: That is also possible for the birds and beasts.

Prof. Dara: But there is a big difference between the talking of birds and beasts and our talking.

Śrīla Prabhupāda: What is the difference? They are talking in their community, and you are talking in your community.

Prof. Dürckheim: I believe the real point is that the animal has no self-consciousness. He does not understand what he is in essence.

Reincarnation means that I am a spirit soul who has entered a body. But in my next life I will enter another body. It may be a dog's body, it may be a cat's body, or it may be a king's body. (*p. 33*)

Rising Above the Beasts

Śrīla Prabhupāda: Yes, that is the real point. A human being can understand what he is. The birds and beasts cannot understand. So, as humans, we should endeavor for self-realization and not simply act on the level of the birds and beasts. Therefore the *Vedānta-sūtra* begins with the aphorism *athāto brahma-jijñāsā*—human life is meant for inquiring about the Absolute Truth. That is the aim of human life, not eating and sleeping like the animals. We possess extra intelligence with which to understand the Absolute Truth. In *Śrīmad-Bhāgavatam* [1.2.10] it is said,

kāmasya nendriya-prītir
lābho jīveta yāvatā
jīvasya tattva jijñāsā
nārtho yaś ceha karmabhiḥ

"Life's desires should never be directed toward sense gratification. One should desire only a healthy life, or self-preservation, since a human being is meant for inquiry about the Absolute Truth. Nothing else should be the goal of one's works."

Prof. Dara: But is it just a waste of time to use our bodies to do good to others?

Śrīla Prabhupāda: You cannot do good to others, because you do not know what good is. You are thinking of good in terms of the body—but the body is false in the sense that you are not the body. For instance, you might occupy an apartment, but you are not that apartment. If you simply decorate the apartment and forget to eat, can that be good?

Prof. Dara: I don't think this comparison of the body with a room is very good—

Śrīla Prabhupāda: That's because you don't know that you are not the body.

Prof. Dara: But if we go out of a room, the room remains. When we go out of the body, it doesn't remain.
Śrīla Prabhupāda: Eventually the room will also be destroyed.
Prof. Dara: What I mean to say is that there must be a very intimate connection between the body and the soul, a kind of oneness—at least, as long as we are alive.
Śrīla Prabhupāda: No; that is not real oneness. There is a difference. For instance, the room we are presently in is important to me only as long as I am alive. Otherwise, it has no importance. When the soul leaves the body, the body is thrown away, even though it was very dear to its owner.
Prof. Dara: But what if you don't want to leave your body?
Śrīla Prabhupāda: It is not a question of what you want. You must leave. As soon as your death comes, your relatives will throw out your body.
Prof. Dürckheim: Perhaps it makes a difference if a person thinks "I am the spirit and I have a body" rather than "I am the body and I have a soul."

The Secret of Immortality

Śrīla Prabhupāda: Yes. It is a mistake to think that you are the body and possess a soul. That is not true. You *are* the soul, and you are covered by a temporary body. The soul is the important thing, not the body. For example, as long as you wear a coat, it is important to you. But if it becomes torn, you throw it away and purchase another coat. The living being constantly experiences the same thing. You separate from this present body and accept another body. That is called death. The body which you previously occupied becomes unimportant, and the body you now occupy becomes important. This is the big problem—people give so much importance to a body that within a few short years will be exchanged for another one.

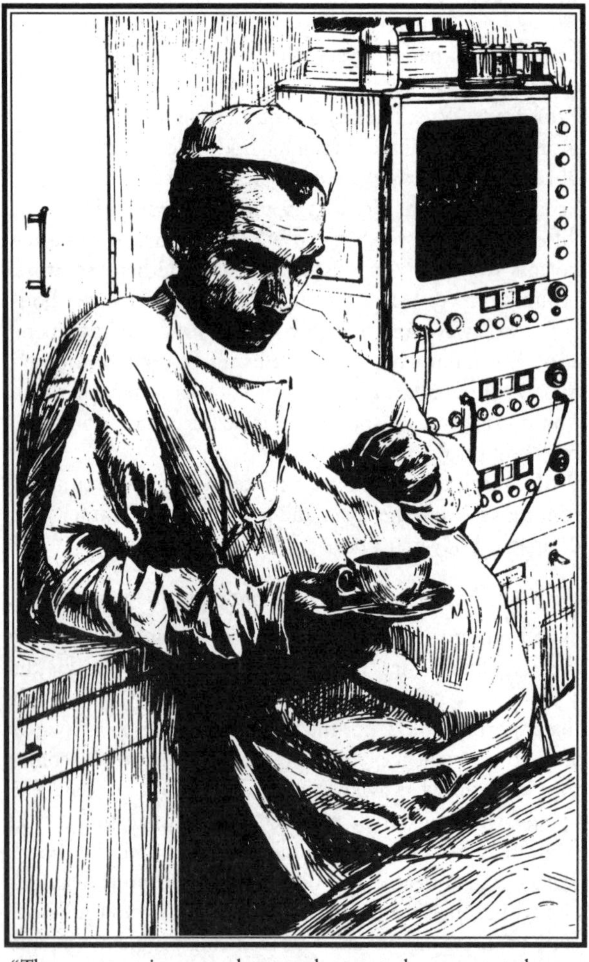

"There are certain cases where you happen to be present at the moment when people pass from a living state to death, and some mysterious changes take place." (*p. 40*)

3

Soul Research

Although advanced in understanding the mechanical workings of the physical body, modern science gives little attention to analyzing the spiritual spark that animates the body. In the Montreal Gazette *article reproduced below, we find world-famous cardiologist Wilfred G. Bigelow urging systematic research to determine what the soul is and where it comes from. Reproduced next is Śrīla Prabhupāda's letter in response to Dr. Bigelow's plea. Śrīla Prabhupāda presents substantial Vedic evidence about the science of the soul and suggests a practical method for scientifically understanding this spiritual spark that gives the body life and makes reincarnation a reality.*

Montreal Gazette Headline:

Heart Surgeon Wants to Know What a Soul Is

WINDSOR—A world-famous Canadian heart surgeon says he believes the body has a soul which departs at death and says theologians ought to try to find out more about it.

Dr. Wilfred G. Bigelow, head of the cardiovascular surgery unit at Toronto General Hospital, said that "as a person who believes there is a soul," he thought the time had come "to take the mystery out of this and find out what it is."

Bigelow was a member of a panel which appeared before

the Essex County Medical-Legal Society to discuss problems associated with attempts to define the exact moment of death.

The question has become vital in the age of transplants of hearts and other organs in cases when the donors are inevitably dying.

The Canadian Medical Association has produced a widely accepted definition of death as the moment when the patient is in coma, responds to no stimulus of any kind, and brain waves recorded on a machine are flat.

The other members of the panel were Justice Edson L. Haines of the Ontario Supreme Court and J. Francis Leddy, president of the University of Windsor.

Bigelow, elaborating on points he had raised during the discussion, said in an interview later that his thirty-two years as a surgeon had left him no doubts that there is a soul.

"There are certain cases where you happen to be present at the moment when people pass from a living state to death, and some mysterious changes take place.

"One of the most noticeable is the sudden lack of life or luster to the eyes. They become opaque and literally lifeless.

"It's difficult to document what you observe. In fact, I don't think it can be documented very well."

Bigelow, who became world renowned for his pioneering work in the "deep freeze" surgical technique known as hypothermia and for his heart valve surgery, said "soul research" should be undertaken by theology and allied disciplines within the university.

During this discussion Leddy said that "if there is a soul, you are not going to see it. You are not going to find it."

"If there is a principle of vitality or life, what is it?" The problem is that "the soul doesn't exist anywhere specifically, geographically. It's everywhere and yet it's nowhere in the body."

"It would be nice to start experimenting, but I don't know how you are going to get data on any of these things," Leddy said. He said the discussion reminded him of the Soviet cosmonaut who returned from space to report there was no God, because he didn't see Him up there.

Maybe so, said Bigelow, but in modern medicine when something was encountered that could not be explained, "the watchword is discover the answer, take it into the laboratory, take it somewhere where you can discover the truth."

The central question, said Bigelow, is "where is the soul and where does it come from?"

Śrīla Prabhupāda Presents the Vedic Evidence

My dear Dr. Bigelow:

Please accept my greetings. I recently read an article in the *Gazette* by Rae Corelli entitled "Heart Surgeon Wants to Know What a Soul Is" and found it very interesting. Your comments show great insight, so I thought to write you on this matter. Perhaps you may know that I am the founder-*ācārya* of the International Society for Krishna Consciousness. I have several temples in Canada—Montreal, Toronto, Vancouver, and Hamilton. This Kṛṣṇa consciousness movement is specifically meant to teach every soul his original, spiritual position.

Undoubtedly the soul is present in the heart of the living entity, and it is the source of all the energies which maintain the body. The energy of the soul is spread all over the body, and this is known as consciousness. Since this consciousness spreads the energy of the soul all over the body, one feels pains and pleasures in every part of the body. The soul is individual, and he transmigrates from one body to another, just as a person transmigrates from boyhood to youth, and then to advanced old age. Death takes place when we change to a new body, just as we change from our old dress to a new dress. This is called transmigration of the soul.

When a soul wants to enjoy this material world, forgetting his real home in the spiritual world, he takes this life of hard struggle for existence. This unnatural life of repeated birth, death, disease, and old age can be stopped when his consciousness is dovetailed with the supreme consciousness of God. That is the basic principle of the Kṛṣṇa consciousness movement.

As far as heart transplants are concerned, there is no question of success unless the recipient's soul enters into the transplanted heart. So the presence of the soul must be accepted. In sexual intercourse, if there is no soul, there is no conception, no pregnancy. Contraception deteriorates the womb so that it is no longer a good place for the soul. That is against the order of God. By the order of God a soul is sent to a particular womb, but by contraceptive methods he is denied that womb and has to be placed in another. That is disobedience to the Supreme. For example, take a man who is supposed to live in a particular apartment. If the situation there is so disturbed that he cannot enter the apartment, then he is put at a great disadvantage. That constitutes illegal interference and is punishable by law.

The undertaking of "soul research" would certainly mark the advancement of science. But no matter how much science advances, they will not be able to find the soul. The soul's presence can simply be accepted on circumstantial understanding, for you will find in the Vedic literature that the dimension of the soul is one ten-thousandth the size of a point. Therefore, it is not possible for the material scientists to capture the soul. You can simply accept the soul's existence by taking it from higher authorities. What the greatest scientists are now finding to be true, we've explained long ago.

As soon as one understands the existence of the soul, he can immediately understand the existence of God. The difference between God and the soul is that God is a very great soul and the living entity is a very small soul, but qualitatively they are equal. God is all-pervading and the living entity is localized, but the nature and quality are the same.

The central question, you say, is "Where is the soul, and where does it come from?" That is not difficult to understand. We have already discussed how the soul is residing in the heart of the living entity and how it takes shelter in another body after death. Originally the soul comes from God. Just as a spark that comes from a fire appears to be extinguished when it falls away from the fire, the spark of the soul originally comes from the spiritual world to the material world. In the material world the soul falls down into three different conditions called the modes of nature—or goodness, passion, and ignorance. When a spark of fire falls on dry grass, the fiery quality continues; when the spark falls on the ground, it cannot display its fiery manifestation unless some combustible materials are present; and when the spark falls on water, it is extinguished. In this way, we find the soul takes up three kinds of living conditions. One living entity is completely forgetful of his spiritual nature, another is almost forgetful but still has an instinct of spiritual nature, and another is completely in search of spiritual perfection. There is a bona fide method for the attainment of spiritual perfection by the spiritual spark, or soul, and if he is properly guided, he is very easily sent back home, back to Godhead, from where he originally fell.

It will be a great contribution to human society if this

authorized information from the Vedic literature is presented on the basis of modern scientific understanding. The facts are already there. It simply has to be presented for modern understanding. If the doctors and scientists of the world can help man understand the science of the soul, this will be a great contribution.

Sincerely yours,
A.C. Bhaktivedanta Swami

His Divine Grace
A.C. Bhaktivedanta Swami Prabhupāda
Founder-*Ācārya*
of the International Society for Krishna Consciousness

Socrates

Napoleon

Emerson

Gandhi

Four famous persons who have accepted the truth of reincarnation. (*Chapter 1*)

As the embodied soul continuously passes, in this body, from childhood to youth to old age, the soul similarly passes into another body at death. The purpose of human life is to stop this painful process. (*p. 15*)

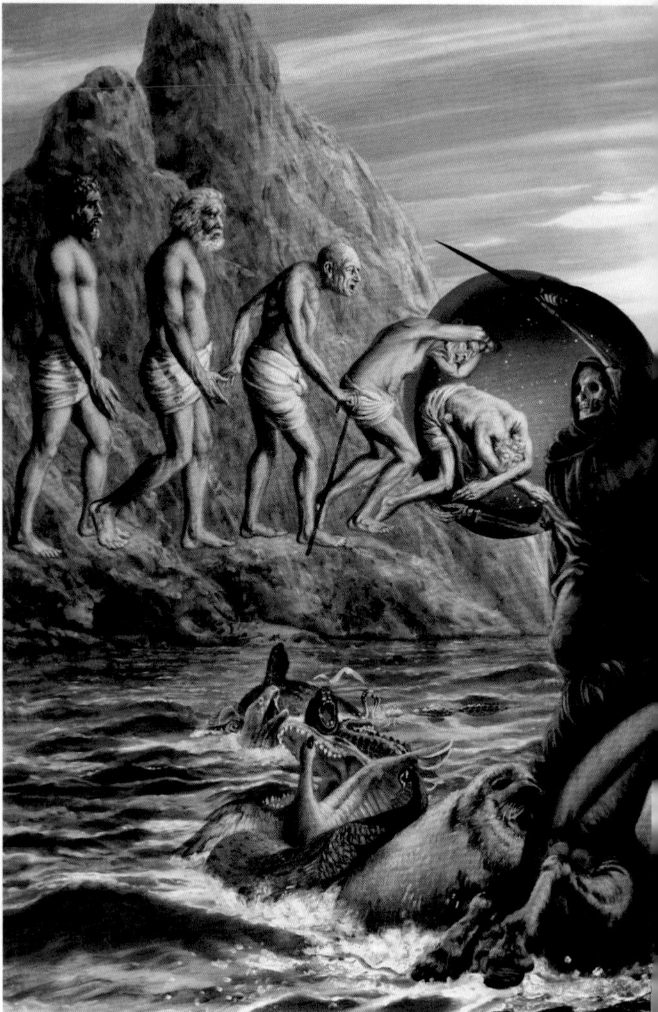

At the time of death the soul enters a new body. There are 8,400,000 species of life, beginning with the aquatics and culminating in the human form of life, which offers the

chance to become free from the cycle of birth and death. If one does not use the human form to achieve liberation, one may descend into the lower species. (*p. 16*)

At the end of Ajāmila's life, three gruesome figures with fierce, twisted faces appeared at his bedside. These were the servants of Yamarāja, the lord of death, and they had come

In this material world, all people become friends, relatives, and enemies in due course of time. But despite these various transactions, no one is permanently related. (*p. 55*)

to claim his soul. But they were forbidden to do so by the servants of Lord Viṣṇu, for with his final breath Ajāmila had chanted the holy name of the Lord. (*p. 76–77*)

The soul of King Citraketu's dead child reentered the boy's body and began to speak to his father and mother about his previous lives. (*p. 54*)

4

Three Histories of Reincarnation

For thousands of years, the greatest spiritual teachers of India have used historical narrations found in Śrīmad-Bhāgavatam, *like the three included here, to illustrate for their disciples the principles of reincarnation.*

Śrīmad-Bhāgavatam, *an epic philosophical and literary classic, holds a prominent position in India's voluminous written wisdom. The timeless knowledge of India is expressed in the* Vedas, *ancient Sanskrit texts that touch upon all fields of human understanding. Known as "the ripened fruit of the tree of Vedic literature,"* Śrīmad-Bhāgavatam *is the most complete and authoritative exposition of Vedic knowledge.*

The scientific principles of reincarnation do not change with the passage of time; they remain constant, and these timeless stories are as relevant to the modern seeker as they were to those who sought enlightenment in bygone ages.

–I–

THE PRINCE WITH A MILLION MOTHERS

Some look on the soul as amazing, some describe him as amazing, and some hear of him as amazing, while others, even after hearing about him, cannot understand him at all.
—*Bhagavad-gītā* 2.29

"Our birth is but a sleep and a forgetting," writes British poet William Wordsworth in his famous "Intimations of Immortality." And in another poem he addresses the following lines to an infant:

Oh, sweet new-comer to the changeful earth,
If, as some darkling seers have boldly guessed,
Thou hadst a being and a human birth,
And wert erewhile by human parents blessed,
Long, long before thy present mother pressed
Thee, helpless stranger, to her fostering breast.

In the following historical narration from *Śrīmad-Bhāgavatam,* King Citraketu's son reveals his previous births and instructs the king and queen about the imperishable nature of the soul and the science of reincarnation.

King Citraketu had many wives, and although he was capable of producing children, he did not receive a child from any of them, for his beautiful wives were all barren.

One day the mystic sage Aṅgirā came to Citraketu's palace. The king immediately stood up from his throne and, as was the Vedic custom, paid his respects.

"O King Citraketu, I can observe that your mind is disturbed. Your pale face reflects your deep anxiety. Have you not achieved your desired goals?" the sage inquired.

Because he was a great mystic, Aṅgirā knew the cause of the king's distress, but for his own reasons he questioned Citraketu, as if in need of knowledge.

King Citraketu replied, "O Aṅgirā, because of your great penances and austerities, you have acquired complete knowledge. You can understand everything, both external and internal, about embodied souls like myself. O great soul, you are aware of everything, yet you ask why I am in such anxiety. Therefore, in response to your question, let me disclose the cause of my suffering. A starving man cannot be satisfied with a garland of flowers. In the same way, my vast empire and immeasurable wealth mean nothing, for I am bereft of a man's true wealth. I do not have a son. Can you not help me become truly happy by arranging for me to have a son?"

Aṅgirā, who was very merciful, agreed to help the king. He performed a special sacrifice to the demigods and then offered the remnants of the sacrificial food to the most perfect of Citraketu's queens, Kṛtadyuti. "O great king, you will now have a son who will be the cause of both jubilation and lamentation," Aṅgirā said. The sage then vanished, without waiting for the King's response.

Citraketu was overjoyed to learn that he would finally get a son, but he wondered about the sage's last words.

"Aṅgirā must have meant that I will be greatly happy when my son is born. That is certainly true. But what did he mean by the child being the cause of lamentation? Of course, being my only son, he will automatically become

the heir to my throne and kingdom. Therefore, he might become proud and disobedient. That might be a cause for lamentation. But a disobedient son is better than no son at all."

In due course of time, Kṛtadyuti became pregnant, and a son was born. Hearing this news, all the inhabitants of the kingdom rejoiced. King Citraketu could not contain his joy.

As the king carefully raised his infant son, his affection for Queen Kṛtadyuti increased daily, and he gradually lost affection for his barren wives. The other queens continuously lamented their fate, for a wife who has no sons is neglected at home by her husband, and her co-wives treat her exactly like a maidservant. The barren queens burned with anger and envy. As their envy increased, they lost their intelligence, and their hearts became hard like stone. They met secretly and decided that there was only one solution to their dilemma, one way to regain the love of their husband: poison the child.

One afternoon, as Queen Kṛtadyuti walked in the courtyard of the palace, she thought of her son sleeping peacefully in his room. Because she loved the child dearly and could hardly bear to be without him for a moment, she ordered the nurse to awaken him from his nap and bring the boy to the garden.

But when the maidservant approached the child, she saw that his eyes were turned upward and there were no signs of life. Horrified, she held a swab of cotton beneath the boy's nostrils, but the cotton did not move. Seeing this, she cried out, "Now I am doomed!" and fell to the ground. In great agitation, she struck her breast with both hands and wept loudly.

Some time passed, and the anxious queen approached the child's bedroom. Hearing the nurse's wailing, she entered the room and saw that her son had passed from this world. In great lamentation, her hair and dress in disarray, the queen fell to the ground unconscious.

When the king heard of his son's sudden death, he became nearly blind with grief. His lamentation grew like a conflagration, and as he ran to see the dead child, he repeatedly stumbled and fell. Surrounded by his ministers and court officers, the king entered the boy's room and collapsed at the child's feet, his hair and clothes scattered in all directions. When he regained consciousness, he was breathing heavily, his eyes were filled with tears, and he was unable to speak.

When the queen saw her husband merged in great lamentation and again viewed the dead child, she began to curse the Supreme Lord. This increased the pain in the hearts of all the residents of the palace. The queen's flower garlands slipped from her body, and her smooth jet-black hair became tangled. Falling tears smeared the cosmetics beneath her eyes.

"O Providence! During the lifetime of the father you have caused the death of his son. You are certainly the enemy of the living beings and are not at all merciful." Turning to her beloved child, she said, "My dear son, I am helpless and aggrieved. You should not give up my company. How can you leave me? Just look at your lamenting father! You have slept for a long time. Now *please* get up. Your playmates are calling you to play. You must be very hungry, so please get up immediately and take your lunch. My dear son, I am most unfortunate, for I can no longer see your sweet smiling. You have closed your eyes forever. You have been taken from this planet to another place, from which you will not return. My dear son, unable to hear your pleasing voice, I can no longer maintain my life."

The king began crying loudly with an open mouth As

the mother and father lamented, all their followers joined them, bemoaning the untimely death of the child. Because of the sudden accident, all the citizens of the kingdom were nearly unconscious with grief.

When the great sage Aṅgirā understood that the king was almost dead in an ocean of sorrow, he went there with his friend, Saint Nārada.

The two sages found the king, overwhelmed by lamentation, lying like a dead body beside the corpse. Aṅgirā addressed him sharply, "Wake up from the darkness of ignorance! O king, what relationship does this dead body have with you, and what relationship do you have with him? You may say that you are now related as father and son, but do you think that this relationship existed before his birth? Does it truly exist now? Will it continue now that he is dead? O king, as small particles of sand sometimes come together and are sometimes separated due to the force of the ocean's waves, living entities who have accepted material bodies sometimes come together and are sometimes separated by the force of time." Aṅgirā wanted the king to understand that all bodily relationships are temporary.

"My dear king," the sage continued, "when I first came to your palace, I could have given you the greatest gift—transcendental knowledge—but when I saw that your mind was absorbed in material things, I gave you only a son, who caused you jubilation and lamentation. Now you are experiencing the misery of a person who has sons and daughters. These visible objects like wife, children, and property are nothing more than dreams. Therefore, O King Citraketu, try to understand who you really are. Consider where you have come from, where you are going after giving up this body, and why you are under the control of material lamentation."

Then Nārada Muni did something very wonderful. By his mystic power he brought the soul of the king's dead child into the vision of everyone. Immediately the room became effulgent with a blinding brightness, and the dead child began to move. Nārada said, "O living entity, all good fortune unto you. Just see your father and mother. All your friends and relatives are overwhelmed with grief because of your death. Because you died untimely, the balance of your life still remains. Therefore, you may reenter your body and enjoy the remainder of the years allotted to you in this body with your friends and relatives, and later you may accept the royal throne and all the opulences given by your father."

By Nārada's mystic power, the living entity reentered the dead body. The child who had been dead sat up and began to speak, not with the intelligence of a young boy, but with the full knowledge of a liberated soul. "According to the results of my material activities, I, the living being, transmigrate from one body to another, sometimes going to the species of the demigods, sometimes to the species of lower animals, sometimes incarnating among the vegetables, and sometimes appearing in the human species. In which birth were these two people my father and mother? No one is actually my father and mother. I have had millions of so-called parents. How can I accept these two people as my father and mother?"

The *Vedas* teach that the eternal living being enters a body made of material elements. Here we find that such a living being entered a body produced by King Citraketu and his wife. Actually, however, he was not their son. The living entity is the eternal son of the Supreme Personality of Godhead, but because he wants to enjoy this material world, God gives him a chance to enter various bodies. Yet the pure living being has no true relationship with the material body he gets from his father and mother. Therefore, the soul who had taken the body of Citraketu's son flatly denied that the king and queen were his parents.

The soul continued, "In this material world, which is like a swiftly flowing river, all people become friends, relatives, and enemies in due course of time. They also act neutrally and in many other relationships. But despite these various transactions, no one is permanently related."

Citraketu was lamenting for his son, who was now dead, but he could have considered the situation otherwise. "This living entity," he could have thought, "was my enemy in my last life, and now, having appeared as my son, he is prematurely leaving just to give me pain and agony." Why should the king not consider his dead son his former enemy and instead of lamenting be jubilant because of an enemy's death?

The living being in the body of Citraketu's child said, "Just as gold and other commodities are continually transferred from one place to another through buying and selling, so the living entity, as a result of his karma, wanders throughout the universe, being injected into various bodies in different species of life through the semen of one father after another."

As explained in the *Bhagavad-gītā,* it is not by any father or mother that the living entity is given birth. The living entity's true identity is completely separate from the so-called father and mother. By the laws of nature, the soul is forced to enter the semen of a father and be injected into the womb of a mother. He cannot directly control the kind of father he will get; this is automatically determined by his activities in previous lives. The laws of karma force him to go to different fathers and mothers, just like a commodity that is bought and sold.

The living entity sometimes takes shelter of an animal

father and mother and sometimes a human father and mother. Sometimes he accepts a father and mother among the birds, and sometimes he accepts a demigod father and mother in the heavenly planets.

As the soul transmigrates through different bodies, everyone, in every form of life—be it human, animal, tree, or demigod—gets a father and mother. This is not very difficult. The real difficulty is to obtain a *spiritual* father—a bona fide spiritual master. Therefore, the duty of a human being is to search out such a spiritual master, for under his guidance one can become free from the cycle of reincarnation and return to his original home in the spiritual world.

"The living being is eternal," the pure soul continued, "and has no relation with so-called fathers and mothers. He falsely accepts himself as their son and acts affectionately. After he dies, however, the relationship is finished. Under these circumstances, one should not be falsely involved with jubilation and lamentation. The living entity is eternal and imperishable, he has no beginning and no end, nor does he take birth or die. The living being is equal in quality to the Supreme Lord. Both are spiritual personalities. But because the living entity is so small, he is prone to be illusioned by the material energy, and thus he creates bodies for himself according to his different desires and activities."

The *Vedas* tell us that the soul is responsible for his lives in the material world, where he is trapped in the cycle of reincarnation, material body after material body. If he likes, he can remain suffering in the prison house of material existence, or he can return to his original home in the spiritual world. Although God arranges through the material energy to give the living beings the bodies they desire, the Lord's true desire is that the conditioned souls get off the punishing merry-go-round of material life and return home, back to Godhead.

Suddenly the boy became silent as the pure soul left the body of the child and the body fell lifeless to the floor. Citraketu and the other relatives were astonished. They cut the shackles of their affection and gave up their lamentation. Then they performed the funeral ceremony, cremating the body. Queen Kṛtadyuti's co-wives, who had poisoned the child, were very much ashamed. While lamenting, they remembered the instructions of Aṅgirā and gave up their ambition to bear children. Following the directions of the *brāhmaṇa* priests, they went to the bank of the sacred river Yamunā, where they bathed and prayed daily, atoning for their sinful activities.

Because King Citraketu and his queen had become fully cognizant of spiritual knowledge, including the science of reincarnation, they easily gave up the affection that leads to pain, fear, grief, and illusion. Although this attachment for the material body is very difficult to overcome, because they severed it with the sword of transcendental knowledge, they were able to give it up very easily.

"Because this deer has taken shelter of me, how can I neglect it? Even though it is disturbing my spiritual life, I cannot ignore it."
(*p. 62*)

-II-

A VICTIM OF AFFECTION

As a person puts on new garments, giving up old ones, the soul similarly accepts new material bodies, giving up the old and useless ones.

—*Bhagavad-gītā* 2.22

In the first century B.C., the Roman poet Ovid penned these verses describing the fate of an unfortunate person who, by his actions and desires, slid a few notches down the evolutionary scale.

I am ashamed to tell you, but I will tell—
I had bristles sprouting on me.
I could not speak, but only grunting sounds
Came out instead of words.
I felt my mouth grow harder.
I had a snout instead of a nose,
And my face bent over to see the ground.
My neck swelled up with great muscles,
And the hand that lifted the cup to my lips
Made footprints on the ground.

—*Metamorphoses*

Śrīmad-Bhāgavatam, composed some three thousand years before Ovid's time, contains the following unique story that dramatically reveals the principles of reincarnation in action. India's great and pious monarch, King Bharata, due to his extreme attachment to a deer, had to spend one life in a deer's body before again attaining a human form.

King Bharata was a wise and experienced *mahārāja* who one might have thought would rule for hundreds of years. But while in the prime of life, he renounced everything—his queen, family, and vast empire—and went to the forest. In so doing, he was following the advice of the great sages of ancient India, who recommend that one devote the latter part of one's life to self-realization.

King Bharata knew that his position as a great monarch was not permanent; therefore, he did not try to keep the royal throne until death. After all, even a king's body ultimately becomes dust, ashes, or food for worms and other animals. But within the body is the imperishable soul, the real self. Through the process of yoga, the self can be awakened to its true spiritual identity. Once this occurs, the soul need not spend another term of imprisonment within a material body.

Understanding that the real purpose of life is to free oneself from the cycle of reincarnation, King Bharata journeyed to a sacred place of pilgrimage called Pulaha-āśrama, in the foothills of the Himalayas. There the former king lived alone in the forest along the bank of the Gaṇḍakī River. Instead of his royal dress, he now wore only a deerskin garment. His hair and beard grew long and matted and always appeared wet because he bathed three times a day in the river.

Each morning Bharata worshiped the Supreme Lord by chanting the hymns given in the *Ṛg Veda,* and as the sun rose he recited the following mantra: "The Supreme Lord is situated in pure goodness. He illuminates the entire universe; by virtue of His different potencies He maintains all living beings desiring material enjoyment, and He bestows all benediction upon His devotees."

Later in the day he collected various fruits and roots, and as recommended in the Vedic scriptures, he offered these simple edibles to Lord Kṛṣṇa, the Supreme Personality of Godhead, and then took them for his food. Even though he had been a great king, surrounded by worldly opulence, now, by the strength of his austerities, all his desires for material enjoyment vanished. Thus he became free of the root cause of bondage in the cycle of birth and death.

By his constant meditation upon the Personality of Godhead, Bharata began to experience symptoms of spiritual ecstasy. His heart was like a lake filled with the water of ecstatic love, and when his mind bathed itself in that lake, tears of joy flowed from his eyes.

One day while Bharata was meditating near the bank of the river, a doe came there to drink. While she drank, a lion in the forest nearby roared loudly. The doe was pregnant, and as she jumped in great fear and ran from the river, a baby deer fell from her womb into the swiftly flowing waters. The doe, shivering in fright and weak from the miscarriage, entered a cave, where she soon died.

As the sage observed the fawn floating down the river, he felt great compassion. Bharata lifted the animal from the water and, knowing it to be motherless, brought it to his āśrama. Bodily differences are meaningless from the viewpoint of a learned transcendentalist: because Bharata was self-realized, he saw all living beings with equal vision, knowing that both the soul and the Supersoul (Supreme Lord) are present within the bodies of all. He daily fed the deer with fresh green grass and tried to make it comfortable. Soon, however, he began to develop great attachment for the deer; he lay down with it, walked with it, bathed with it, and even ate with it. When he wanted to enter the forest to collect fruits, flowers, and roots, he would take the deer with him, fearing that if he left it behind, it would be killed by dogs, jackals, or tigers. Bharata took great pleasure seeing the deer leap and frolic in the forest like a child. Sometimes he would carry the fawn on his shoulders. His heart was so filled with love for the deer that he would keep it on his lap during the day, and when he slept, the deer would rest upon his chest. He was forever petting the deer and would sometimes even kiss it. Thus his heart became bound to the deer in affection.

Being attached to raising the deer, Bharata gradually became neglectful of his meditation upon the Supreme Lord. He thus became distracted from the path of self-realization, which is the actual goal of human life. The *Vedas* remind us that the human form is obtained only after the soul undergoes millions of births in lower species of life. This material world is sometimes compared to an ocean of birth and death, and the human body is compared to a solid boat designed to cross this ocean. The Vedic scriptures and the saintly teachers, or spiritual masters, are compared to expert boatmen, and the facilities of the human body are compared to favorable breezes that help the boat ply smoothly to its desired destination. If, with all these facilities, a person does not fully utilize his life for self-realization, then he commits spiritual suicide and risks taking his next birth in an animal body.

However, even though Bharata was aware of these considerations, he thought to himself, "Because this deer has taken shelter of me, how can I neglect it? Even though it is disturbing my spiritual life, I cannot ignore it. To neglect a helpless person who has taken shelter of me would be a great fault."

One day, as Bharata was meditating, he began, as usual, to think of the deer instead of the Lord. Breaking his concentration, he glanced around to see where the deer was, and when he could not discover it, his mind became agitated, like that of a miser who has lost his money. He got up and searched the area around his āśrama, but the deer was nowhere to be found.

Bharata thought, "*When will my deer return? Is it safe from tigers and other animals? When shall I again see it wandering in my garden, eating the soft green grasses?*"

As the day wore on and the deer still did not return, Bharata became overwhelmed with anxiety. "*Has my deer been eaten by a wolf or a dog? Has it been attacked by a herd of wild boars, or by a tiger who travels alone? The sun is now setting, and the poor animal who has trusted me since its mother died has not yet returned.*"

He remembered how the deer would play with him, touching him with the points of its soft, fuzzy horns. He remembered how he would sometimes push the deer away from him, pretending to be annoyed with it for disturbing his worship or meditation, and how it would then immediately become fearful and sit down motionless a short distance away.

"My deer is exactly like a little prince. Oh, when will he again return? When will he again pacify my wounded heart?"

Unable to restrain himself, Bharata set out after the deer, following its tiny hoofprints in the moonlight. In his madness, he began to talk to himself: "*This creature was so dear to me that I feel as though I have lost my own son. Due to the burning fever of separation, I feel as if I were in the middle of a blazing forest fire. My heart is now blazing with distress.*"

While frantically searching for the lost deer along the dangerous forest paths, Bharata suddenly fell and was fatally injured. Lying there at the point of death, he saw that his deer had suddenly appeared and was sitting at his side, watching over him just like a loving son. Thus, at the moment of his death, the king's mind was focused completely on the deer. In the *Bhagavad-gītā* we learn that "Whatever state of being one remembers when he quits his body, that state he will attain without fail."

King Bharata Becomes a Deer

In his next life King Bharata entered the body of a deer. Most living entities are not able to remember their past lives, but because of the spiritual progress the king had made in his previous incarnation, he could, even though in the body of a deer, understand the cause of his taking birth in that body. He began to lament. "What a fool I was! I have fallen from the path of self-realization. I gave up my family and kingdom and went to a solitary holy place in the forest to meditate, where I always contemplated the Lord of the universe. But due to my foolishness, I let my mind become attached to—of all things—a deer. And now I have justly received such a body. No one is to blame but myself."

But even as a deer, Bharata, having learned a valuable lesson, was able to continue his progress in self-realization. He became detached from all material desires. He no longer cared for the succulent green grasses, nor did he give a thought to how long his antlers would grow. Similarly, he gave up the company of all deer, male and female alike, leaving his mother in the Kālañjara Mountains, where he had been born. He returned to Pulaha-āśrama, the very place where he had practiced meditation in his previous life. But this time he was careful never to forget the Supreme Personality of Godhead. Staying near the hermitages of the great saints and sages, and avoiding all contact with materialists, he lived very simply, eating only hard, dry leaves. When the time of death came and Bharata was leaving the body of the deer, he loudly uttered the following prayer: "The Supreme Personality of Godhead is the source of all knowledge, the controller of the entire creation, and the Supersoul within the heart of every living being. He is beautiful and attractive. I am quitting this body offering obeisances unto Him and hoping that I may perpetually engage in His transcendental loving service."

The Life of Jaḍa Bharata

In his next life King Bharata took birth in the family of a pure, saintly *brāhmaṇa* priest and was known as Jaḍa Bharata. By the Lord's mercy he could again remember his past lives. In the *Bhagavad-gītā* Lord Kṛṣṇa says, "From Me come remembrance, knowledge, and forgetfulness." As he grew up, Jaḍa Bharata became very much afraid of his friends and relatives because they were very materialistic and not at all interested in making spiritual progress. The boy was in constant anxiety, for he feared that by their influence he would again fall down into animal life. Therefore, although he was very intelligent, he behaved just like a madman. He pretended to be dull, blind, and deaf so that mundane people would not try to talk to him. But within himself he was always thinking of the Lord and chanting His glories, which alone can save one from repeated birth and death.

Jaḍa Bharata's father was filled with affection for his son, and in his heart he hoped that Jaḍa Bharata would someday become a learned scholar. Therefore he tried to teach him the intricacies of Vedic knowledge. But Jaḍa Bharata purposely behaved like a fool so that his father would abandon his attempts to instruct him. If his father told him to do something, he would do exactly the opposite. Nevertheless, Jaḍa Bharata's father, until the time of his death, always tried to instruct the boy.

Jaḍa Bharata's nine half brothers considered him dull and brainless, and when their father died, they abandoned all attempts to educate him. They could not understand Jaḍa

Bharata's inner spiritual advancement. But Jaḍa Bharata never protested their mistreatment, for he was completely liberated from the bodily concept of life. Whatever food came his way, he would accept it and eat, whether it was much or little, palatable or unpalatable. Since he was in full transcendental consciousness, he was not disturbed by material dualities like heat and cold. His body was as strong as a bull's, and his limbs were very muscular. He didn't care for winter's cold, summer's heat, wind, or rain. Because his body was perpetually dirty, his spiritual knowledge and effulgence were covered, just like a valuable gem covered by dirt and grime. Each day he was insulted and neglected by ordinary people, who considered him to be nothing more than a useless fool.

Jaḍa Bharata's only wages were the small portions of unpalatable food provided by his brothers, who made him work like a slave in the fields. But he was unable to perform even simple tasks satisfactorily, because he did not know where to spread dirt or where to make the ground level. For food, his brothers gave him broken rice, rice chaff, oil cakes, worm-eaten grains, and burned grains that had stuck to the bottom of the cooking pots, but Jaḍa Bharata gladly accepted all this as if it were nectar. And he never held any grudges. He thus displayed the symptoms of a perfectly self-realized soul.

Once a leader of a band of thieves and murderers went to the temple of the goddess Bhadrakālī to offer in sacrifice a dull, unintelligent human being resembling an animal. Such sacrifices are nowhere mentioned in the *Vedas* and were concocted by the robbers for the purpose of gaining material wealth. Their plan was foiled, however, when the man who was to have been sacrificed escaped, so the chief robber sent his henchmen out to find him. Searching through fields and forests in the darkness of night, the robbers came to a rice field and saw Jaḍa Bharata, who was sitting on high ground guarding the field against the attacks of wild boars. The robbers thought Jaḍa Bharata would be a perfect sacrifice. Their faces shining with happiness, the robbers bound him with strong ropes and brought him to the temple of the goddess Kālī. Jaḍa Bharata, because of his complete faith in the protection of the Supreme Lord, did not protest. There is a song by a famous spiritual master that reads, "My Lord, I am now surrendered unto You. I am Your eternal servant, and if You like You can kill me, or if You like You can protect me. In any case, I am fully surrendered unto You."

The robbers bathed Jaḍa Bharata, dressed him in new silk garments, and decorated him with ornaments and garlands. They fed him a sumptuous last meal and brought him before the goddess, whom they worshiped with songs and prayers. Jaḍa Bharata was forced to sit before the deity. Then, one of the thieves, acting as the chief priest, raised a razor-sharp sword to slit Jaḍa Bharata's throat so they could offer Kālī his warm blood as liquor.

But the goddess could not bear this. She understood that the sinful thieves were about to kill a great devotee of the Lord. Suddenly, the form of the deity burst open and the goddess herself appeared, her body burning with an intense, intolerable effulgence. The infuriated goddess flashed her blazing eyes and displayed her fierce, curved teeth. Her eyes, crimson orbs, glowered, and she appeared as if she were prepared to destroy the entire cosmos. Leaping violently from the altar, she quickly decapitated all the rogues and thieves with the very sword with which they had intended to kill the saint Jaḍa Bharata.

Jaḍa Bharata Instructs King Rahūgaṇa

After his escape from the Kālī temple, Jaḍa Bharata continued his wanderings, remaining aloof from ordinary, materialistic men.

One day, as King Rahūgaṇa of Sauvīra was being carried through the district on a palanquin resting on the shoulders of several servants, the men, who were fatigued, began to falter. Realizing they would need another carrier to help them cross the Ikṣumatī River, the king's servants began searching for someone. Soon they saw Jaḍa Bharata, who appeared to be a good choice because he was very young and strong as an ox. But because he saw all living beings as his brothers, Jaḍa Bharata could not perform this task very well. As he walked, he kept stopping to be sure that he wasn't stepping on any ants. According to the subtle but precise laws of reincarnation, all living entities must remain for a specific length of time in a particular body before being promoted to a higher form. When an animal is killed before its time, the soul must return to that same species to complete its encagement in that type of body. Therefore, the *Vedas* enjoin that one should always avoid whimsically killing other living beings.

Unaware of what was causing the delay, King Rahūgaṇa shouted, "What's going on? Can't you carry this thing properly? Why is my palanquin shaking like this?"

Hearing the threatening voice of the king, the frightened servants replied that the disturbance was being caused by Jaḍa Bharata. The king angrily chastised him, sarcastically accusing Jaḍa Bharata of carrying the palanquin like a weak, skinny, tired old man. But Jaḍa Bharata, who understood his true spiritual identity, knew that he was not his body. He was neither fat nor thin, nor did he have anything to do with the lump of flesh and bones that comprised his body. He knew that he was an eternal spirit soul situated within the body, like a driver within a machine. Therefore, Jaḍa Bharata remained unaffected by the king's angry criticism. Even if the king were to order him killed, he would not have cared, because he knew that the soul is eternal and can never be killed. As Lord Kṛṣṇa says in the *Gītā*, "The soul is not slain when the body is slain."

Jaḍa Bharata remained silent and kept carrying the palanquin as before, but the king, unable to control his temper, shouted, "You rascal, what are you doing? Don't you know that I am your master? For your disobedience I shall now punish you!"

"My dear king," said Jaḍa Bharata, "whatever you have said about me is true. You seem to think that I have not labored hard enough to carry your palanquin. That is true, because actually I am not carrying your palanquin at all! My body is carrying it, but I am not my body. You accuse me of not being very stout and strong, but this merely shows your ignorance of the spirit soul. The body may be fat or thin, weak or strong, but no learned man would say such things about the real self within. As far as my soul is concerned, it is neither fat nor skinny; therefore you are correct when you say that I am not very strong."

Jaḍa Bharata then began to instruct the king, saying, "You think you are lord and master, and you are therefore trying to command me, but this is also incorrect, because these positions are ephemeral. Today you are a king and I am your servant, but in our next lives our positions may be reversed; you may be my servant and I your master."

Just as the waves of the ocean bring pieces of straw together and then break them apart, the force of eternal time brings living entities together in temporary relationships, such as master and servant, and then breaks them apart and rearranges them.

"In any case," Jaḍa Bharata continued, "who is master and who is servant? Everyone is forced to act by the laws of material nature; therefore no one is master and no one is servant."

The *Vedas* explain that the human beings in this material

world are like actors on a stage, performing under the direction of a superior. Onstage, one actor may play the role of a master and another the role of his servant, but they are both actually the servants of the director. In the same way, all living entities are the servants of the Supreme Lord, Śrī Kṛṣṇa. Their roles as masters and servants in the material world are temporary and imaginary.

After explaining all this to King Rahūgaṇa, Jaḍa Bharata said, "If you still think that you are the master and I am the servant, I shall accept this. Please order me. What can I do for you?"

King Rahūgaṇa, who had been trained in spiritual science, was astonished to hear the teachings of Jaḍa Bharata. Recognizing him as a saintly person, the king quickly descended from his palanquin. His material conception of himself as a great monarch had been obliterated, and he fell humbly to the ground, his body outstretched, offering obeisances, his head at the feet of the holy man.

"O saintly person, why are you moving through the world unknown to others? Who are you? Where do you live? Why have you come to this place? O spiritual master, I am blind to spiritual knowledge. Please tell me how I may advance in spiritual life."

King Rahūgaṇa's behavior is exemplary. The *Vedas* declare that everyone, even kings, must approach a spiritual master to gain knowledge of the soul and the process of reincarnation.

Jaḍa Bharata replied, "Because his mind is full of material desires, the living entity takes on different bodies in this material world, to enjoy and suffer the pleasures and pains brought about by material activity."

When one sleeps at night, one's mind creates many dreamlike situations of enjoyment and suffering. A man may dream that he is associating with a beautiful woman, but this enjoyment is illusory. He may also dream that he is being chased by a tiger, but the anxiety he experiences is also unreal. In the same way, material happiness and distress are simply mental creations, based on identification with the material body and material possessions. When one awakens to his original, spiritual consciousness, he sees that he has nothing to do with these things. One accomplishes this by concentrating one's mind in meditation upon the Supreme Lord.

One who fails to constantly fix his mind on the Supreme Lord and render service to Him must undergo the cycle of birth and death described by Jaḍa Bharata.

"The condition of the mind causes births in different types of bodies," Jaḍa Bharata said. "These bodies may be those of many different species, for when one uses the mind to understand spiritual knowledge, he gets a higher body, and when one uses it only for obtaining material pleasure, he receives a lower body."

Jaḍa Bharata compared the mind to a flame in a lamp. "When the flame burns the wick improperly, the lamp is blackened with soot. But when the lamp is filled with clarified butter and the flame burns properly, the lamp produces brilliant illumination. The mind absorbed in material life brings endless suffering in the cycle of reincarnation, but when the mind is used to cultivate spiritual knowledge, it brings about the original brightness of spiritual life."

Jaḍa Bharata then warned the King, "As long as one identifies with the material body, one must wander throughout the unlimited universes in different species of life. Therefore, the uncontrolled mind is the greatest enemy of the living being.

"My dear King Rahūgaṇa, as long as the conditioned soul accepts the material body and is not freed from the contamination of material enjoyment, and as long as he does not conquer his senses and his mind and come to the platform of self-realization by awakening his spiritual knowledge, he is forced to wander in different places and in different forms in this material world."

Jaḍa Bharata then revealed his own past lives. "In a previous birth I was known as King Bharata. I attained perfection by becoming completely detached from material activities. I was fully engaged in the service of the Lord, but I relaxed my control over my mind and became so affectionate to a small deer that I neglected my spiritual duties. At the time of death I could think of nothing but this deer, so in my next life I had to accept the body of a deer."

Jaḍa Bharata concluded his teachings by informing the King that those who desire freedom from the cycle of reincarnation must always associate with self-realized devotees of the Lord. Only by associating with exalted devotees can one attain the perfection of knowledge and cut to pieces the illusory associations of this material world.

Unless one has the opportunity to get the association of the devotees of the Lord, he can never understand the first thing about spiritual life. The Absolute Truth is revealed only to one who has attained the mercy of a great devotee, because in the assembly of pure devotees there is no question of discussing material subjects like politics and sociology. In an assembly of pure devotees there is discussion only of the qualities, forms, and pastimes of the Supreme Personality of Godhead, who is praised and worshiped with full attention. This is the simple secret by which one can revive his dormant spiritual consciousness, end forever the vicious cycle of reincarnation, and return to a life of eternal pleasure in the spiritual world.

After receiving lessons from the great devotee Jaḍa Bharata, King Rahūgaṇa became fully aware of the constitutional position of the soul and completely gave up the bodily conception of life, which chains the inherently pure soul to the endless cycle of birth and death in the material world.

The servants of Lord Viṣṇu saw the servants of the lord of death snatching Ajāmila's soul from the core of his heart, and they cried, "Stop!" (*pp.* 76–77)

-III-

VISITORS FROM BEYOND

Whatever state of being one remembers when he quits his body, that state he will attain without fail.

—*Bhagavad-gītā* 8.6

As the soul sets out on its mysterious journey after death, it may, according to the traditions of the world's great religions, meet with beings from other levels of reality—angels who help it, or judges who weigh its good and evil deeds on the scales of cosmic justice. A variety of religious art objects, spanning the entire range of man's cultural history, depict such scenes. A painting on a fragment of Etruscan pottery shows an angelic figure attending a fallen warrior. A Christian mosaic from the Middle Ages shows a grim St. Michael, the scales of justice in his hands. Many people who have had near-death experiences often report encountering such beings.

In the Vedic scriptures of India we learn of the servants of Lord Viṣṇu, who appear at the time of death to accompany the pious soul on its way to the spiritual world. The *Vedas* also tell of the fearsome agents of Yamarāja, the lord of death, who forcefully arrest the soul of a sinful man and prepare it for its next incarnation in the prison of a material body. In this historical account, the servants of Viṣṇu and the servants of Yamarāja dispute the fate of the soul of Ajāmila, deciding whether he should be liberated or reincarnated.

In the city of Kānyakubja, there once lived a young saintly *brāhmaṇa* priest named Ajāmila, who fell from the path of spiritual life and lost all his good qualities when he fell in love with a prostitute. Giving up his priestly duties, Ajāmila now made his living through robbery and gambling and passed his life in debauchery.

By the time he was eighty-eight years old, Ajāmila had fathered ten sons by the prostitute. The youngest, a baby, was named Nārāyaṇa—one of the names of the Supreme Lord, Viṣṇu. Ajāmila was very attached to his young son and derived great pleasure watching the child's early attempts to walk and talk.

One day, without warning, the time of death arrived for the foolish Ajāmila. Terrified, the old man saw before him gruesome figures with fierce, twisted faces These subtle beings with ropes in their hands had come to forcibly escort him to the court of Yamarāja, the lord of death. Seeing these ghoulish creatures, Ajāmila became bewildered, and out of affection for his beloved child, who was playing a short distance away, he began to cry loudly, "Nārāyaṇa! Nārāyaṇa!" With tears in his eyes, weeping for his young son, the great sinner Ajāmila unwittingly chanted the holy name of the Lord.

Hearing their master's name chanted with great feeling by the dying Ajāmila, the order carriers of Viṣṇu, the Viṣṇudūtas, arrived within a second. They appeared just like Lord Viṣṇu Himself. Their eyes resembled the petals of a lotus flower; they wore helmets of burnished gold and glittering yellow silk garments; and their perfectly formed bodies were decorated with garlands of fragrant lotuses. They appeared fresh and youthful, and their dazzling effulgence illuminated the darkness of the death chamber. In their hands they held bows, arrows, swords, conchshells, clubs, discs, and lotus flowers.

The Viṣṇudūtas saw the servants of Yamarāja, the Yamadūtas, snatching Ajāmila's soul from the core of his heart, and with resounding voices they cried, "Stop!"

The Yamadūtas, who had never before encountered any opposition, trembled upon hearing the Viṣṇudūtas' harsh command. "Who are you? Why are you trying to stop us?" they asked. "We are the servants of Yamarāja, the lord of death."

The agents of Viṣṇu smiled and spoke in voices as deep as the rumbling of rain clouds: "If you are truly the servants of Yamarāja, you must explain to us the meaning of the cycle of birth and death. Tell us: Who must enter this cycle, and who must not?"

The Yamadūtas replied, "The sun, fire, sky, air, demigods, moon, evening, day, night, the directions, water, land, and the Supersoul, or the Lord within the heart, all witness the activities of everyone. The candidates for punishment in the cycle of birth and death are those who are confirmed by these witnesses to have deviated from their religious duties. In proportion to the extent of one's religious or irreligious actions in this life, one must enjoy or suffer the corresponding reactions of karma in the next."

Originally the living beings exist in the spiritual world as eternal servants of God. But when they give up the service of the Lord, they must enter the material universe, comprised of the three modes of nature—goodness, passion, and ignorance. The Yamadūtas explained that the living beings who desire to enjoy this material world come under the control of the modes and, according to their specific relationship with these modes, acquire suitable material bodies. A being in the mode of goodness obtains the body of a demigod, one in the mode of passion takes birth as a human, and one in the mode of ignorance enters the lower species.

All of these bodies are like the bodies we experience in dreams. When a man goes to sleep, he forgets his real identity and may dream that he has become a king. He cannot remember what he was doing before he went to sleep, nor can he imagine what he will do upon waking. In the same way, when a soul identifies with a temporary, material body, he forgets his real, spiritual identity, as well as any previous lives in the material world, although most souls in a human body have already transmigrated through all 8,400,000 species of life.

"The living entity thus transmigrates from one material body to another in human life, animal life, and life as a demigod," the Yamadūtas said. "When the living entity gets the body of a demigod, he is very happy. When he gets a human body, he is sometimes happy and sometimes sad. And when he gets the body of an animal, he is always fearful. In all conditions, however, he suffers terribly, experiencing birth, death, disease, and old age. His miserable condition is called *saṁsāra,* or transmigration of the soul through different species of material life.

"The foolish embodied living entity," the Yamadūtas continued, "unable to control his senses or his mind, is forced to act according to the influence of the modes of material nature, even against his own desires. He is like a silkworm that uses its own saliva to create a cocoon and then becomes trapped in it. The living entity traps himself in a network of his own fruitive activities and then can find no way to free himself. Thus he is always bewildered and repeatedly dies and is reborn.

"Because of his intense material desires," said the Yamadūtas, "a living entity takes birth in a particular family and receives a body like that of either the mother or the father. That body is an indication of his past and future bodies, just as one springtime is an indication of past and future springtimes."

The human form of life is especially valuable, because only a human being can understand the transcendental knowledge that can free him from the cycle of birth and death. But Ajāmila had wasted his human life.

"In the beginning," the Yamadūtas said, "Ajāmila studied all the Vedic literatures. He was a reservoir of good character and conduct. He was very mild and gentle, and he kept his mind and senses under control. He was always truthful, knew how to chant the Vedic mantras, and was very pure. Ajāmila always showed proper respect to his spiritual master, guests, and the elderly members of his household—indeed, he was free from false prestige. He was benevolent to all living beings and never envied anyone.

"But once, following the order of his father, Ajāmila went to the forest to collect fruits and flowers. On the way home he came upon a very lusty low-class man shamelessly embracing and kissing a prostitute. The man was smiling, singing, and enjoying himself as if this were proper behavior. Both the man and the prostitute were drunk. The prostitute's eyes were rolling in intoxication, and her dress had become loose, partially exposing her body. When Ajāmila saw the prostitute, the dormant lusty desires in his heart awakened, and in illusion he fell under their control. He tried to remember the instructions of the scriptures and control his lust with the help of his knowledge and intellect. But because of the force of Cupid within his heart, he was unable to control his mind. After that, he always thought of the prostitute, and within a short time he took her in as a servant in his house.

"Ajāmila then gave up all of his spiritual practices. He spent the money he had inherited from his father on presents for the prostitute and even rejected his beautiful young wife, who came from a respectable *brāhmaṇa* family.

"This rascal Ajāmila got money any way he could, legally or illegally, and used it to maintain the prostitute's sons and daughters. Before death, he did not undergo atonement.

Therefore, because of his sinful life, we must take him to the court of Yamarāja. There, according to the extent of his sinful acts, he will be punished and then returned to the material world in a suitable body."

After hearing the statements of the Yamadūtas, the servants of Lord Viṣṇu, who are always expert in logic and argument, replied, "How painful it is to see that those in charge of upholding religious principles are needlessly punishing an innocent person. Ajāmila has already atoned for all his sins. Indeed, he has atoned not only for sins performed in this life but for those performed in millions of previous lives as well, because he chanted the holy name of Nārāyaṇa in a helpless state of mind at the time of death. Therefore, he is now pure and is eligible for liberation from the cycle of reincarnation.

"The chanting of the holy name of Lord Viṣṇu," the Viṣṇudūtas said, "is the best process of atonement for a thief or a drunkard, for one who betrays a friend or relative, for one who kills a priest, or for one who indulges in sex with the wife of his guru or another superior. It is also the best method of atonement for one who murders women, the king, or his father, for one who slaughters cows, and for all other sinful persons. Simply by chanting the holy name of Lord Viṣṇu, such sinful persons may attract the attention of the Supreme Lord, who therefore considers, 'Because this person has chanted My holy name, it is My duty to give him protection.'"

In this present age of quarrel and hypocrisy, one who wants liberation from reincarnation should chant the Hare Kṛṣṇa *mahā-mantra,* the great *mantra* of deliverance, because it completely cleanses the heart of all material desires that keep one trapped in the cycle of birth and death.

The Viṣṇudūtas said, "One who chants the holy name of the Lord is immediately freed from the reactions of unlimited sins, even if he chants jokingly or for musical entertainment. This is accepted in the scriptures and by all learned scholars.

"If one chants the holy name of Lord Kṛṣṇa and then dies in an accident or from a disease or is killed by a weapon or a deadly animal, one is immediately freed from having to take birth again. As a fire burns dry grass to ashes, the holy name of Kṛṣṇa burns to ashes all of one's karmic reactions."

The Viṣṇudūtas then said, "If a person unaware of the potency of a medicine takes that medicine or is forced to take it, it will act even without his knowledge. Even if one does not know the value of chanting the holy name of the Lord, the chanting will still be effective in liberating one from reincarnation.

"At the time of death," said the Viṣṇudūtas, "Ajāmila helplessly and very loudly chanted the holy name of the Lord, Nārāyaṇa. That chanting alone has already freed him from having to take birth again for his sinful life. Therefore, do not try to take him to your master for punishment and for imprisonment in another material body."

The Viṣṇudūtas then released Ajāmila from the ropes of the servants of the lord of death. Ajāmila came to his senses and, free from fear, paid his heartfelt respects to the Viṣṇudūtas by bowing his head at their feet. But when the Viṣṇudūtas saw that Ajāmila was trying to say something to them, they disappeared.

"Was this a dream I saw?" Ajāmila wondered. "Or was it reality? I saw fearsome men with ropes in their hands coming to drag me away. Where have they gone? And where are those four radiant persons who saved me?"

Ajāmila then began to reflect on his life. "Being a servant of my senses, how degraded I became! I fell down from my position as a saintly *brāhmaṇa* and begot children in the womb of a prostitute. Indeed, I gave up my chaste and beautiful young wife. What's more, my father and mother were old and had no other friend or son to look after them. Because I did not take care of them, they lived with great pain and difficulty. It is now clear that a sinful person like myself should have been forced in his next life to suffer hellishly.

"I am such an unfortunate person," said Ajāmila, "but now that I have another chance, I must try to become free from the vicious cycle of birth and death."

Ajāmila immediately renounced his prostitute wife and journeyed to Hardwar, a place of pilgrimage in the Himalaya Mountains. There he took shelter at a Viṣṇu temple, where he practiced *bhakti-yoga,* the *yoga* of devotional service to the Supreme Lord. When his mind and intelligence were fixed in perfect meditation on the form of the Lord, Ajāmila again saw before him four celestial beings. Recognizing them as the same Viṣṇudūtas who had saved him from the agents of death, he bowed down before them.

There at Hardwar, on the banks of the Ganges, Ajāmila gave up his temporary material body and regained his eternal spiritual form. Accompanied by the Viṣṇudūtas, he boarded a golden aircraft and, passing through the airways, went directly to the abode of Lord Viṣṇu, never again to reincarnate in this material world.

That subtle forms exist in the ether has been proven by modern science by transmission of television waves, by which forms or photographs in one place are transmitted to another place by the action of the ethereal element. (*p. 91*)

5

The Soul's Secret Journey

(Excerpts from the writings of
His Divine Grace
A.C. Bhaktivedanta Swami Prabhupāda)

One Life Is Just a Flash in Time

From time immemorial the living entity travels in the different species of life and the different planets, almost perpetually. This process is explained in the *Bhagavad-gītā:* under the spell of *māyā,* everyone is wandering throughout the universe on the carriage of the body offered by the material energy. Materialistic life involves a series of actions and reactions. It is a long film spool of actions and reactions, and one life span is just a flash in such a reactionary show. When a child is born, it is to be understood that his particular type of body is the beginning of another set of activities, and when an old man dies, it is to be understood that one set of reactionary activities is finished.

Śrīmad-Bhāgavatam (3.31.44)

You Get the Body of Your Choice

The living entity creates his own body by his personal desires, and the external energy of the Lord supplies him with the exact form by which he can enjoy his desires to the fullest extent. The tiger wanted to enjoy the blood of another animal; therefore, by the grace of the Lord, the material energy supplied him the body of the tiger, with facilities for enjoying blood from another animal.

Śrīmad-Bhāgavatam (2.9.2)

Death Means Forgetting Your Last Life

After death one forgets everything about the present bodily relationships; we have a little experience of this at night when we go to sleep. While sleeping, we forget everything about this body and bodily relations, although this forgetfulness is a temporary situation for only a few hours. Death is nothing but sleeping for a few months in order to develop another term of bodily encagement, which we are awarded by the law of nature according to our aspiration. Therefore, one has only to change the aspiration during the course of this present body, and for this there is need of training in the current duration of human life. This training can be begun at any stage of life, or even a few seconds before death, but the usual procedure is for one to get the training from very early life.

Śrīmad-Bhāgavatam (2.1.15)

The Soul Takes a Human Form First

Originally the living entity is a spiritual being, but when he desires to enjoy this material world, he comes down. We can understand that the living entity first accepts a body that is human in form, but gradually, due to his degraded activities, he falls into lower forms of life—into the animal, plant, and aquatic forms. By the gradual process of evolution, the living entity again attains the body of a human being and is given another chance to get out of the process of transmigration. If he again misses his chance in the human form to understand his position, he is again placed in the cycle of birth and death in various types of bodies.

Śrīmad-Bhāgavatam (4.29.4)

The Science of Reincarnation Is Unknown to Modern Scientists

This science of transmigration is completely unknown to modern scientists. So-called scientists do not like to bother with these things because if they would at all consider this subtle subject matter and the problems of life, they would see that their future is very dark.

Śrīmad-Bhāgavatam (4.28.21)

Ignorance of Reincarnation Is Dangerous

Modern civilization is based on family comforts, the highest standard of amenities, and therefore after retirement everyone expects to live a very comfortable life in a well-furnished home decorated with fine ladies and children, without any desire to get out of such a comfortable home. High government officers and ministers stick to their prize posts until death, and they neither dream nor desire to get out of homely comforts. Bound by such hallucinations, materialistic men prepare various plans for a still more comfortable life, but suddenly cruel death comes without mercy and takes away the great planmaker against his desire, forcing him to give up the present body for another body. Such a planmaker is thus forced to accept another body in one of the 8,400,000 species of life, according to the fruits of the work he has performed.

In the next life, persons who were too much attached to family comforts are generally awarded lower species of life on account of sinful acts performed during a long duration of sinful life, and thus all the energy of the human life is spoiled. In order to be saved from the danger of spoiling the human form and being attached to unreal things, one must take warning of death at the age of fifty, if not earlier. The principle is that one should take it for granted that the death warning is already there, even prior to the attainment of fifty years of age, and thus at any stage of life one should prepare himself for a better next life.

Śrīmad-Bhāgavatam (2.1.16)

"And Unto Dust Thou Shalt Return"

When we die, this material body composed of five elements—earth, water, air, fire, and ether—decomposes, and the gross materials return to the elements. Or, as the Christian Bible says, "Dust thou art, and unto dust thou shalt return." In some societies the body is burned, in others it is buried, and in others it is thrown to animals. In India, the Hindus burn the body, and thus the body is transformed into ashes. Ash is simply another form of earth. Christians bury the body, and after some time in the grave, the body eventually turns to dust, which again, like ash, is another form of earth. There are other societies—like the Parsee community in India—that neither burn nor bury the body, but throw it to the vultures, and the vultures immediately come to eat the body, and then the body is eventually transformed into stool. So in any case, this beautiful body, which we are soaping and caring for so nicely, will eventually turn into either stool, ashes, or dust. At death, the finer elements (mind, intelligence, and ego) carry the small particle of spirit soul to another body to suffer or enjoy, according to one's work.

The Path of Perfection (p. 101)

Astrology and Reincarnation

Astrological calculations of stellar influences upon a living

Bound by hallucinations, materialistic men prepare plans for a still more comfortable life, but suddenly cruel death comes without mercy and takes away the great planmaker against his desire. (*p. 87*)

being are not suppositions, but are factual, as confirmed in *Śrīmad-Bhāgavatam.* Every living being is controlled by the laws of nature at every minute, just as a citizen is controlled by the influence of the state. The state laws are grossly observed, but the laws of material nature, being subtle to our gross understanding, cannot be experienced grossly.

The law of nature is so subtle that every part of our body is influenced by the respective stars, and a living being obtains his working body to fulfill his terms of imprisonment by the manipulation of such astrological influences. A man's destiny is therefore ascertained by the birth time constellation of stars, and a factual horoscope is made by a learned astrologer. It is a great science, and misuse of a science does not make it useless.

This suitable arrangement of astral influences is never a creation of man's will, but is the arrangement of the superior management of the agency of the Supreme Lord. Of course, the arrangement is made according to the good or bad deeds of the living being. Herein lies the importance of pious acts performed by the living being. Only by pious acts can one be allowed to get good wealth, good education, and beautiful features.

Śrīmad-Bhāgavatam (1.12.12)

[*Editors' note: The term "learned astrologer" in this selection refers to one fully learned in the exacting Vedic science of astrology, in comparison with which modern popular astrology is a foolish exercise in sentimentality compounded with error.*]

Your Thoughts Create Your Next Body

That subtle forms exist in the ether has been proven by modern science by transmission of television waves, by which forms or photographs of one place are transmitted to another place by the action of the ethereal element. Within the *Śrīmad-Bhāgavatam* is the potential basis of great scientific research work, for it explains how subtle forms are generated from the ethereal element, what their characteristics and actions are, and how the tangible elements, namely air, fire, water, and earth, are manifested from the subtle form. Mental activities, or psychological activities of thinking, feeling, and willing, are also activities on the platform of ethereal existence. The statement in *Bhagavad-gītā* that the mental situation at the time of death is the basis of the next birth is also corroborated in many places in the *Bhāgavatam*. Mental existence transforms into tangible form as soon as there is an opportunity.

Śrīmad-Bhāgavatam (3.26.34)

Why Some People Can't Accept Reincarnation

There is life after death, and there is also the chance to free oneself from the cycle of repeated birth and death and attain a life of immortality. But because we have been accustomed to accepting one body after another since time immemorial, it is difficult for us to think of a life that is eternal. And the life of material existence is so troublesome that one may think that if there is an eternal life, that life must be troublesome also. For example, a diseased man who is taking very bitter medicine and who is lying down in bed, eating there and passing stool and urine there, unable to move, may find his life so intolerable that he thinks, "Let me commit suicide." Similarly, materialistic life is so miserable that in desperation one sometimes takes to a philosophy of voidism or impersonalism to try to negate his very existence and make everything zero. Actually, however, becoming zero is not possible, nor is it necessary. We are in trouble in our material condition, but when we get out of our material condition we can find real life, eternal life.

Teachings of Queen Kuntī (p. 107)

Just a Few More Years!

Karma is the aggregate fruitive activities conducted to make this body comfortable or uncomfortable. We have actually seen that when one man was about to die he requested his physician to give him a chance to live four more years so that he could finish his plans. This means that while dying he was thinking of his plans. After his body was destroyed, he doubtlessly carried his plans with him by means of the subtle body, composed of mind, intelligence, and ego. Thus he would get another chance by the grace of the Supreme Lord, the Supersoul, who is always within the heart. In the next birth, one acquires remembrance from the Supersoul and begins to execute plans begun in the previous life. Situated on the vehicle given by material nature and reminded by the Supersoul within the heart, the living entity struggles all over the universe to fulfill his plans.

Śrīmad-Bhāgavatam (4.29.62)

Sex Change Without Surgery

A man gets his next life's birth according to what he thinks of at the time of death. If someone is too attached to his wife, naturally he thinks of his wife at the time of death, and in his next life he takes the body of a woman. Similarly, if a woman thinks of her husband at the time of death, naturally she gets the body of a man in her next life.

We should always remember, as it is stated in *Bhagavad-gītā,* that both the gross and subtle material bodies are dresses; they are the shirt and coat of the living entity. To be either a woman or a man involves only one's bodily dress.

Śrīmad-Bhāgavatam (3.31.41)

Dreams and Past Lives

In dreams we sometimes see things that we have never experienced in the present body. Sometimes in dreams we think that we are flying in the sky, although we have no experience of flying. This means that once in a previous life, either as a demigod or astronaut, we flew in the sky. The impression is there in the stockpile of the mind, and it suddenly expresses itself. It is like fermentation taking place in the depths of water, which sometimes manifests itself in bubbles on the water's surface. Sometimes we dream of coming to a place we have never known or experienced in this lifetime, but this is proof that in a past life we experienced this. The impression is kept within the mind and sometimes becomes manifest either in dream or in thought. The conclusion is that the mind is the storehouse of various thoughts and experiences undergone during our past lives. Thus there is a chain of continuation from one life to another, from previous lives to this life, and from this life to future lives.

Śrīmad-Bhāgavatam (4.29.64)

Comas and the Next Life

A living entity too much absorbed in material activity becomes very much attached to the material body. Even at the point of death, he thinks of his present body and the relatives connected to it. Thus he remains fully absorbed in the bodily conception of life, so much so that even at the point of death he abhors leaving his present body. Sometimes it is found that a person on the verge of death remains in a coma for many days before giving up the body.

A person may be enjoying the body of a prime minister or a president, but when he understands that he will be forced to accept the body of a dog or hog, he chooses not to leave the present body. Therefore he lies in a coma many days before death.

Śrīmad-Bhāgavatam (4.29.77)

Ghosts and Suicide

Ghosts are bereft of a physical body because of their grievously sinful acts, such as suicide. The last resort of ghostly characters in human society is to take shelter of suicide, either material or spiritual. Material suicide causes loss of the physical body, and spiritual suicide causes loss of the individual identity.

Śrīmad-Bhāgavatam (3.14.24)

Changing Bodies: Reflections of Māyā

The moon is stationary and is one, but when it is reflected in water or oil, it appears to take different shapes because of the movements of the wind. Similarly, the soul is the eternal servant of Kṛṣṇa, the Supreme Personality of Godhead, but when put into the material modes of nature, it takes different bodies, sometimes as a demigod, sometimes a man, a dog, a tree, and so on. By the influence of *māyā,* the illusory potency of the Supreme Personality of Godhead, the living entity thinks that he is this person, that person, American, Indian, cat, dog, tree, or whatever. This is called *māyā.* When one is freed from this bewilderment and understands that the soul does not belong to any shape of this material world, one is situated on the spiritual platform. As soon as the living entity returns to his original, spiritual form and understanding, he immediately surrenders to the supreme form, the Personality of Godhead.

Śrīmad-Bhāgavatam (10.1.43)

Politicians Are Reborn in Their Countries

At the time of death, every living entity worries about what will happen to his wife and children. Similarly, a politician also worries about what will happen to his country or his political party. A politician or so-called nationalist who is inordinately attached to the land of his birth will certainly be reborn in the same land after ending his political career. One's next life will also be affected by the acts one performs during this life. Sometimes politicians act most sinfully for their own sense gratification. It is not unusual for a politician to kill the opposing party. Even though a politician may be allowed to take birth in his so-called homeland, he still has to undergo suffering due to his sinful activities in his previous life.

Śrīmad-Bhāgavatam (4.28.21)

What's Wrong with Animal Killing?

Ahiṁsā [nonviolence] means not arresting the progressive life of any living entity. One should not think that since the spiritual spark is never killed even after the killing of the body there is no harm in killing animals for sense gratification. People are now addicted to eating animals, in spite of having an ample supply of grains, fruits, and milk. There is no necessity for animal killing. . . .The animals are also making progress in their evolutionary life by transmigrating from one category of animal life to another. If a particular animal is killed, then his progress is checked. If an animal is staying in a particular body for so many days or so many years and is untimely killed, then he has to come back again in that form of life to complete the remaining days in order to be promoted to another species of life. So their progress should not be checked simply to satisfy one's palate.

Bhagavad-gītā As It Is (16.1–3)

Evolution: The Soul's Journey Through the Species

We see that there are so many forms. Where do these different forms come from—the form of the dog, the form of the cat, the form of the tree, the form of the reptile, the forms of the insects, the forms of the fish?

There may be evolution, but at the same time all the different species are existing. The fish is existing, the man is existing, the tiger is existing, everyone is existing.

It is just like the different types of apartments in any city. You may occupy one of them according to your ability to pay the rent, but all types of apartments are nevertheless existing at the same time. Similarly, the living entity, according to his karma, is given facility to occupy one of these bodily forms. But there is evolution also. From the fish, the next stage of evolution is to plant life. From plant forms, the living entity may enter an insect body. From the insect body, the next stage is bird, then beast, and finally the spirit soul may evolve to the human form of life. And from the human form, if one becomes qualified, he may evolve further. Otherwise, he must again enter the evolutionary cycle. Therefore, this human form of life is an important junction in the evolutionary development of the living entity.

Consciousness: The Missing Link (p.5)

Māyā's Illusion

Māyā's *illusion is like the foam*
Which mixes again with the sea.

No one is mother, father, or relative;
Like the sea foam, they remain a short while only.
And, as the sea foam merges into the sea,
This precious body of five elements disappears.
Who can say how many ephemeral forms
The embodied soul has taken?

Bengali poem
by His Divine Grace
A.C. Bhaktivedanta Swami
Prabhupāda

A gluttonous person who indiscriminately gorges himself on vast and varied quantities of victuals may be offered by material nature the body of a pig or goat. (*p. 101*)

6

The Logic of Reincarnation

Has it occurred to you that transmigration is at once an explanation and a justification of the evil of the world? If the evils we suffer are the result of sins committed in our past lives, we can bear them with resignation and hope that if in this one we strive toward virtue our future lives will be less afflicted.

—W. Somerset Maugham
The Razor's Edge

Two children are born at the same time on the same day. The parents of the first are wealthy and well educated and have anxiously awaited the arrival of their firstborn for years. Their child, a boy, is bright, healthy, and attractive, with a future full of promise. Surely destiny has smiled upon him.

The second child enters into an entirely different world. He is born to a mother who was abandoned while pregnant. In her poverty she feels little enthusiasm to rear her sickly new offspring. The road ahead is fraught with difficulties and hardships, and to rise above them will not be easy.

The world is full of disparities like these, blatant inequalities that often provoke questions: "How could Providence be so unfair? What did George and Mary do to have their son born blind? They're good people. God is so unkind!"

The principles of reincarnation, however, allow us to view life with a much broader perspective—from the standpoint of eternity. From this point of view, one brief lifetime is seen not as the beginning of our existence, but as nothing more than a flash in time, and we can understand that an apparently pious person who may be suffering greatly is reaping the effects of impious activities performed in this or previous lives. With this broader vision of universal justice we can see how each individual soul is alone responsible for his own karma.

Our actions are compared to seeds. Initially they are performed, or planted, and over the course of time they gradually fructify, releasing their resultant reactions. Such reactions may produce either suffering or enjoyment for the living being, and he may respond by either improving his character or by becoming increasingly animallike. In either case, the laws of reincarnation operate impartially to award each living being the destiny he has earned by his previous actions.

A criminal chooses to enter prison by willful transgression of the law, but another man may be appointed to sit on the Supreme Court by dint of his excellence of service. In the same way, the soul chooses his own destiny, including the selection of a specific physical form, based on past and present desires and actions. No one can truthfully lament, "I didn't ask to be born!" In the scheme of repeated births and deaths in this material world, "man proposes and God disposes."

Just as a person selects an automobile based on personal driving needs and purchasing power, we ourselves determine, by our own desires and actions, what kind of body material nature will arrange for us next. If a human being wastes this valuable form of life, which is meant only for self-realization, by engaging solely in the animal activities

in his present life, then in his next life he is allowed to continue from that point. The Lord tells his disciple Arjuna in the *Bhagavad-gītā*, "In this endeavor [Kṛṣṇa consciousness] there is no loss or diminution, and a little advancement on this path can protect one from the greatest type of fear [returning in a lower-than-human form in the next life]." The soul may thus develop his inherent spiritual qualities through many lives, until he no longer has to reincarnate in a material body and returns to his original home in the spiritual world.

This is the special benediction of human life—even if one is destined to suffer terribly for impious acts performed in this and previous lives, one can, by taking up the process of Kṛṣṇa consciousness, change his karma. The soul in a human body stands at the evolutionary midpoint. From here the living being can choose either degradation, or liberation from reincarnation.

Past-life hypnotic regressions are at best rudimentary attempts to explain the highly complex phenomenon of reincarnation. (*p. 111*)

7

Almost Reincarnation

The living entity, who has received his present body because of his past fruitive activity, may end the results of his actions in this life, but this does not mean that he is liberated from bondage to material bodies. The living entity receives one type of body, and by performing actions with that body he creates another. Thus he transmigrates from one body to another, through repeated birth and death, because of his gross ignorance.

—*Śrīmad-Bhāgavatam* 7.7.47

Sensationalistic U.S. weekly tabloids are rife with unscientific notions about reincarnation, presenting "startling new evidence" practically every week. And more and more paperback books claiming to tell the "real truth" about past lives glut the market. But who to believe? And what to believe? Can the *National Enquirer* and other similar publications really be accepted as authorities on the science of reincarnation?

Out-of-body experiences are one tangential aspect of reincarnation that has been widely publicized. While many of these out-of-body reports may well be true, they do not provide us with any really new information. Reports of such occurrences may help to convince readers that there is indeed another reality beyond the body—consciousness, or the soul. But this is not new information, for this knowledge has been available for years. The *Vedas* explain that consciousness is a symptom of the soul and therefore has a separate existence from the body. From even a cursory study of the more than five-thousand-year-old *Bhagavad-gītā* and other Vedic literatures, the existence of the soul as distinct from the body becomes obvious. It is not surprising to a student of Vedic science to hear that the soul, carried by the subtle body (consisting of mind, intelligence, and false ego), may temporarily go beyond its material tabernacle during dreams or near-death experiences. False ego means accepting the body as oneself. The sense of "I am" is ego, but when the soul becomes contaminated or conditioned by matter, he identifies with the body and thinks that he is a product of material nature. When the sense of self is applied to reality, or the soul, that is real ego.

Reincarnation: The Real Out-of-Body Experience

Out-of-body experiences (OBEs) are really nothing new. Everyone has had them, for dreams are nothing less than an out-of-body experience. During sleep we enter the dream state when our subtle body leaves the gross form and experiences a different reality on the subtle plane. The subtle body is the vehicle which carries the soul out of the body and into another, new body at the time of death.

A fairly common type of OBE has been documented in cases of near death, when subjects describe how they seemed to hover above their own bodies at the scene of an accident or over the operating table, observing their own bodies without feeling physical pain or discomfort, although many had been declared clinically dead.

Even while the gross body is inactive, the subtle body is active. As already noted, the subtle body sometimes carries us into dreams while our gross body lies sleeping in bed. A similar phenomenon occurs when we go on mental journeys during the day, as in daydreams.

In special circumstances, during a close brush with death, people enter a state researchers have termed the "near-death experience" (NDE). In some cases the terms NDE and OBE can be used interchangeably. During an NDE, the subtle body often hovers above the corporeal form. Since the soul is the elemental principle of life—the very essence of life itself—it can observe the body it belongs to. It can see, hear, and smell, just as if it possessed all the physical faculties of the body.

When the subtle body hovers above the gross form during an NDE, the body may be compared to a car with the engine left running. The driver of the vehicle has stepped out for a moment, but if he does not return, the car runs out of fuel and the engine ceases to run. Similarly, if the soul does not return and reintegrate itself with the body during an NDE, the person dies, and the subtle body carries the soul to another physical body to begin a new life.

This fact is a fundamental principle expounded throughout the Vedic literature. One of the most famous and oft-quoted verses of the *Bhagavad-gītā* states: "As the embodied soul continuously passes, in this body, from boyhood to youth to old age, the soul similarly passes into another body at death. A sober person is not bewildered by such a change." (Bg. 2.13)

During our lifetime we are unknowingly creating the subtle form of our next physical body. Just as a caterpillar transports itself by taking hold of a second leaf before giving up the first, the living entity begins to prepare its new body before giving up the present one. At the moment of actual death, the soul transmigrates to a new body, rendering the body of its former habitation lifeless. *The soul does not need the body for its existence, but without the presence of the soul, the body is nothing more than a corpse.* This transferral of the soul from one body to another is what we call reincarnation.

Although hundreds of recorded NDEs seem to present ample evidence that the mind and soul can exist while separate from the body, NDEs don't give us any definite information about the soul's final destination at death. Therefore, while literature on near-death experiences can provide us with a basis for accepting reincarnation, it still leaves readers sadly uninformed about the true nature of reincarnation and the destiny of the soul after the death experience.

Hypnotic Regressions Do Not Give Us the Whole Picture

A number of popular books on reincarnation focus on cases of hypnotic regression in which subjects allegedly recall details of a past life or past lives. The first such book to have a wide impact was *The Search for Bridey Murphy,* which became a best-seller in the 1950s. It was serialized in more than fifty newspapers, creating something of a worldwide sensation, and became the prototype for a whole genre of past-life-regression books that have appeared in subsequent decades. But this literature about reincarnation only skims the surface, giving us a bantam view of a vast subject, a view that in many ways can be misleading.

In *The Search for Bridey Murphy,* the author, Morey Bernstein, a skilled hypnotist, regressed his middle-aged American subject, Mrs. Virginia Tighe, to her last "incarnation." This was as a girl named Bridey Murphy, who was born in Ireland in 1798, lived there all her life, and died at age sixty-five in Belfast.

Under hypnosis, Tighe disclosed details of "Bridey's"

childhood home, gave the names of parents, friends, and relatives, and reported many other particulars of her "past life." The book reported that Bridey entered the "spiritual world" at death, only to be reborn again in America in 1923 as Virginia Tighe.

Investigators were able to verify some of the information Tighe supplied about Bridey Murphy, but they also discovered parallels between Tighe's childhood and her description of Bridey Murphy's, given under hypnosis. Research revealed, for example, that at the age of four Tighe had lived with an aunt across the street from a woman named Bridey Murphy. As a result, the Bridey Murphy story is still vigorously debated and shrouded in controversy.

From this and many other, similar cases, we can understand that even the most detailed and descriptive "past-life" memories may be events from the subject's childhood. Psychologists studying these cases have deliberately induced hypnotic states in which subjects come up with plausible yet entirely fictional accounts of their "former incarnations." This isn't to say that all hypnotically-induced past-life accounts are fabrications, but separating genuine memories from unconscious fantasies requires a great deal of effort and is often impossible.

Under hypnosis not only can childhood memories be mistaken for past lives, but also *any* thought—a recollection of stories heard in childhood, books read in the past, or even purely imaginary episodes or situations—can easily be mistaken for real past-life experiences. Therefore, the hypnotic regression approach to reincarnation often operates on shaky ground.

Another common fallacy with past-life regression is the inexplicable gap between the present life and the last incarnation. For example, the subject who thought she was Bridey Murphy claimed to have died in 1864 in her last life, leaving a sixty-year period before her "next incarnation" as Virginia Tighe. The book indicates that during this period the soul of Bridey Murphy lived in the "spiritual world."

According to the principle of reincarnation taught in the *Vedas,* we learn that this is quite impossible. The actual process of reincarnation is that the soul, after leaving a material body at death, enters another womb in some species of life in this or another universe, as directed by the immutable laws of karma and arranged by material nature. After death, the disembodied soul, unhindered by a physical body, is able to travel at the speed of the mind. Therefore, there is a negligible time lapse between leaving one body and entering another. However, only fully self-realized souls can attain the spiritual world, beyond the cycle of reincarnation. This is not possible for the ordinary soul, who is conditioned by life in the material world. Every soul, however, has *the potential to* reach the spiritual world after undergoing the necessary spiritual practices.

As Lord Kṛṣṇa explains in the *Bhagavad-gītā* (4.9), "One who knows the transcendental nature of My appearance and activities does not, upon leaving the body, take his birth again in this material world, but attains My eternal abode, O Arjuna." But the Lord further notes that the great souls alone, who are "yogīs in devotion, never return to this temporary world, which is full of miseries, because they have attained the highest perfection." (Bg. 8.15.)

The laws of karma and reincarnation are so perfectly ordered that when each material body dies, nature has already arranged, exactly according to the soul's cumulative karma, another appropriate material body into which the departed soul will enter and take birth anew.

"Whatever state of being one remembers when he quits his body, . . . that state he will attain without fail." (Bg.

8.6.) A self-realized soul who enters the eternal, spiritual world would certainly have neither an obligation nor a desire to reappear in this temporary material world of birth, death, disease, and old age.

The past-life-regression approach to reincarnation occasionally yields evidence of the fact that the same soul inhabits different bodies at different times, and this knowledge is helpful. Many published cases confirm past-life information revealed by hypnotized subjects to be remarkably accurate. Sometimes these hypnotic regressions elicit demonstrations of deeply felt emotions that are hard to doubt. The work of Ian Stevenson in the United States and Peter Ramster in Australia includes carefully documented reincarnation experiments—in many cases involving independent observers to insure integrity. It is noteworthy that some of their subjects spoke fluently in languages with which, it had been proven, they had had little or no contact throughout their lives. A few even spoke in old dialects no longer extant but which were validated through historical records. Some of Ramster's subjects led him and independent observers to remote dwellings in foreign countries never before visited by their subjects. In several cases these buildings, or their remains, meticulously matched subjects' earlier accounts of their past-life homes, accounts which were taped in Ramster's office before his subjects went abroad to begin the verification phase of the experiment.

These types of careful scientific experiments seem to lead us inevitably to the conclusion that reincarnation exist in some form. Unfortunately, they do not give us any real, in-depth knowledge of how transmigration of the soul actually takes place. Therefore, the past-life regression approach to reincarnation is at best a rudimentary attempt to explain a highly complex phenomenon. Moreover, the sensationalism, oversimplification, and even hucksterism that surround so much of this experimentation (most of which is not scientifically conducted), severely limit the regression method as a viable information source about the innumerable intricacies of reincarnation.

Once a Human, Always a Human?

Another popular reincarnation myth posits that the soul, once attaining a human form, always reincarnates in a human body and never in that of a lower species. We *may* reincarnate as humans, but we could also come back as dogs, cats, hogs, or even lower species. The soul, however, despite entering higher or lower bodies, remains unchanged. In any case, the type of body one gets in his next life will be determined by the type of consciousness one develops in this life and by the immutable law of karma. The *Bhagavad-gītā,* the most authoritative sourcebook on reincarnation, spoken by God Himself, clearly states that "when one dies in the mode of ignorance, he takes birth in the animal kingdom." (Bg. 14.15) There is no scientific or scriptural evidence anywhere for this fanciful "once a human, always a human" notion, which runs contrary to the true principles of reincarnation, principles that have been understood and followed by millions of people since time immemorial.

Death Is Not a Painless Transition

Books that paint a rosy picture of death and assure man of a human birth in the next life are dangerously misleading. The authors attempt to portray death as a beautiful, painless transition, an opportunity to experience growth and to progress to newer and higher dimensions of awareness and tranquillity.

Most chic reincarnation theorists would have us believe that after a brief period of cosmic slumber we will experience a warm, drifting, floating sensation as the soul slowly proceeds toward its next human body. Then, we are told, we enter a cozy human womb, where, protected from cruel outside elements, we lie comfortably curled up until the time when we emerge, freeing ourselves at last from the shelter of our mother.

All of this sounds wonderful, but the harsh truth is that birth and death are odious, agonizing experiences. The great sage Kapila Muni informs his mother about the true nature of the death experience: "In that diseased condition, one's eyes bulge due to the pressure of air from within, and his glands become congested with mucus. He has difficulty breathing, and there is a rattling sound within the throat. . . . He dies most pathetically, in great pain and without consciousness." (*Bhāg.* 3.30.16, 18) The soul is so habituated to living in the body that it must be forced out by the laws of nature at the moment of death. Just as no one likes to be forcibly evicted from his home, the soul naturally resists eviction from the material body. Even the tiniest insects will display the most amazing abilities and techniques for avoiding death when their lives are threatened. But as death is inevitable for all living beings, so are the fear and pain associated with it.

The Vedic literature informs us that only self-realized, liberated souls have the power to experience death without anxiety. This is possible because such highly elevated personalities are completely detached from their temporary bodies, being fixed in the knowledge that they are spirit souls with an eternal, nonmaterial existence, independent of all material bodies. Such great souls remain in a state of continuous spiritual bliss and are not bewildered by bodily pains and changes at the time of death.

But taking birth in the material world is no picnic either. For months the human fetus lies cramped within the darkness of the womb, suffering severely, scorched by the mother's gastric fire, continually jolted by sudden movements, and feeling constant pressure from being contained in the small amnion, or sack, which surrounds the body in the womb. This tight, constricting pocket forces the child's back to arch constantly like a bow. Further, the unborn child is tormented by hunger and thirst and is bitten again and again all over the body by hungry worms in the abdominal cavity. Birth is so excruciating, the *Vedas* say, that the process eradicates any memories of one's past life.

The Vedic literature explains that a human birth is very rare. In other words, most living beings in the material world have assumed nonhuman forms. This happens when the soul, giving up the purpose of human life, namely self-realization, becomes entangled in animalistic desires. It must then take its next birth in the animal or lower-than-animal kingdoms.

Reincarnation theories described in popular literature should be seen for what they are: beliefs, opinions, suppositions, and mere speculations.

The physical universe is governed by laws. The subtle universe is governed by other laws, including the laws of karma and of transmigration of the soul. It is under these subtle but stringent laws of nature, described in the *Bhagavad-gītā* and hundreds of other Vedic literatures, that the actual process of reincarnation operates. These laws did not spring into existence whimsically but function under the control of the supreme controller, Śrī Kṛṣṇa, a fact He confirms in the *Gītā* (9.10): "This material nature . . . is working under My direction. . . . Under its rule this manifestation is created and annihilated again and again."

Fashionable notions about reincarnation may be amusing and appealing, but our own destinies are much too important for us to put our faith in frivolous, grossly simplified, inaccurate, and misleading speculations, no matter how attractive they may seem.

The Vedic literature, on the other hand, has for thousands of years provided comprehensive and practical knowledge about the science of reincarnation. This wisdom makes it possible for intelligent persons to gradually approach higher and higher states of awareness and at last escape completely from the endless cycle of birth and death. This is the real goal of human life.

To free ourselves from the endless repetition of birth and death, we must understand the laws of karma and reincarnation. (*p. 125*)

8

Don't Come Back

The sages of ancient India tell us that the goal of human life is to escape from the endless cycle of reincarnation. "Don't come back," they warn.

All in all, the situation of the living entity caught in the cycle of birth and death is somewhat like that of the Greek hero Sisyphus, the king of Corinth, who once tried to outwit the gods but was sentenced to a no-win fate. He was given the punishment of rolling a massive stone up a hill, but each time the stone reached the summit, it rolled down again, and Sisyphus was forced to endlessly repeat his arduous task. Similarly, when a living entity in the material world ends one life, he must, by the law of reincarnation, begin another one. In each life he works hard to achieve his material goals, but his endeavors always end in failure, and he must begin anew.

Fortunately, we're not Sisyphus, and there is a way out of the cycle of birth and death. The first step is the knowledge that "I am not this body." The *Vedas* declare, *ahaṁ brahmāsmi*: "I am pure spirit soul." And as spirit souls we all have a relationship with the supreme spirit soul, Kṛṣṇa, or God. The individual soul may be compared to a spark emanating from the fire of the Supreme Soul. Just as the spark and the fire are of the same quality, the individual soul is of the same spiritual quality as the Supreme Lord. They share a spiritual nature comprised of eternity, knowledge, and bliss. All living beings originally exist in the spiritual world as transcendental loving servants of God, but when the living entity gives up that relationship, he comes under the control of the material energy. The eternal soul then becomes implicated in the cycle of repeated birth and death, taking different bodies according to his karma.

In order to become free from reincarnation, one must thoroughly understand the law of karma. Karma is a Sanskrit term that defines a law of nature analogous to the modern scientific principle of action and reaction. Sometimes we say, "I had that coming to me." We often instinctively realize that we are somehow responsible for the good and bad things that happen to us, although the exact mechanism escapes us. Students of literature use the term "poetic justice" to describe the unhappy fates of ill-motivated characters. And in the realm of religion, theologians debate the meaning of such aphorisms as "An eye for an eye, a tooth for a tooth" and "As ye sow, so shall ye reap."

But the law of karma goes beyond these vague formulations and aphorisms and encompasses a complete science of action and reaction, especially as it applies to reincarnation. In this life, by our thoughts and actions, we prepare our next body, which may be higher or lower.

The human form of life is very rare; the soul gets a human body only after evolving through millions of lower species. And it is only in the human form that the living entity has the intelligence to understand karmic laws and thus become free from reincarnation. The human body is the only loophole by which one can escape the sufferings of material existence. One who misuses the human form and does not become self-realized is no better than a dog or an ass.

The reactions of karma are like dust covering the mirror of our pure, original spiritual consciousness. This contamination can be removed only by the chanting of the holy name of God, especially the Hare Kṛṣṇa mantra, which is comprised of three Sanskrit names of God—Hare, Kṛṣṇa, and Rāma [pronounced Huh-ray; Krish-na; Rahm-uh]:

Hare Kṛṣṇa, Hare Kṛṣṇa
Kṛṣṇa Kṛṣṇa, Hare Hare
Hare Rāma, Hare Rāma
Rāma Rāma, Hare Hare

The power of this mantra (often called the great chant for deliverance) to free one from karma is described throughout the Vedic literature. *Śrīmad-Bhāgavatam,* the cream of the *Purāṇas,* advises, "Living beings who are entangled in the complicated meshes of birth and death can be freed immediately by even unconsciously chanting the holy name of Kṛṣṇa."

In the *Viṣṇu-dharma* it is said, "This word *Kṛṣṇa* is so auspicious that anyone who chants this holy name immediately gets rid of the resultant actions of sinful activities from many, many births." And the *Kali-santaraṇa Upaniṣad* extols the chanting of the Hare Kṛṣṇa mantra as the best means of achieving liberation in the present degraded age.

In order to be effective, however, the Hare Kṛṣṇa mantra must be received from a bona fide spiritual master in the disciplic succession descending from Lord Kṛṣṇa Himself. It is only by the mercy of such a qualified guru that one can become free from the cycle of birth and death. In the *Caitanya-caritāmṛta* Lord Caitanya, who is God Himself, declares, "According to their karma, all living entities are wandering throughout the entire universe. Some of them are being elevated to the upper planetary systems, and some are going down into the lower planetary systems. Out of many millions of wandering living entities, one who is very fortunate gets an opportunity to associate with a bona fide spiritual master by the grace of Kṛṣṇa."

How can one recognize such a bona fide spiritual master? First of all, he must be situated in the authorized line of succession descending from Lord Kṛṣṇa. Such a genuine spiritual master receives the teachings of Lord Kṛṣṇa through the disciplic chain and simply repeats these teachings, without alteration, just as he has heard them from his own spiritual master. He is not an impersonalist or a voidist but rather a representative of the Supreme Personality of Godhead. Moreover, the bona fide spiritual master is completely free from sinful activity (especially meat-eating, illicit sex, gambling, and intoxication) and is always absorbed in God consciousness, twenty-four hours a day.

Only such a spiritual master can free one from reincarnation. Material existence may be compared to a vast ocean of birth and death. The human form of life is like a boat capable of crossing this ocean, and the spiritual master is the captain of this boat. He gives the disciple directions by which he can regain his original spiritual nature.

At the time of initiation, the spiritual master agrees to accept the remaining karma of the disciple. If the disciple perfectly follows the instructions of the genuine guru, or spiritual master, he becomes free from the cycle of reincarnation.

Śrīla Prabhupāda, the founder-*ācārya* of the International Society for Krishna Consciousness, once wrote, "The guru takes on a very great responsibility. He must guide his disciple and enable him to become an eligible candidate for the perfect position—immortality. The guru must be competent to lead his disciple back home, back to

Godhead." He often guaranteed that if one did nothing more than *śravaṇa,* hear about Kṛṣṇa, the supreme controller and cause of all causes, he would be liberated.

Practical Techniques for Becoming Free from Karma and Reincarnation

Activities of sense gratification, meant only to please one's mind and senses, are the cause of material bondage, and as long as one engages in such fruitive activities, the soul is sure to continually transmigrate from species to species.

Lord Ṛṣabhadeva, an incarnation of Kṛṣṇa, warned, "People are mad after sense gratification. When a person considers sense gratification the aim of life, he certainly becomes mad after materialistic living and engages in all kinds of sinful activity. He does not know that due to his past misdeeds he has already received a body, which, although temporary, is the cause of his misery. Actually, the living entity should not have taken on a material body, but he has been awarded the material body for sense gratification. Therefore, I think it not befitting an intelligent man to involve himself again in the activities of sense gratification, by which he perpetually gets material bodies one after another. As long as one does not inquire about the spiritual values of life, one is defeated and subjected to miseries arising from ignorance. Be it sinful or pious, karma has its resultant actions. If a person is engaged in any kind of karma, his mind is called *karmātmaka,* or colored with fruitive activity. As long as the mind is impure, consciousness is unclear, and as long as one is absorbed in fruitive activity, he has to accept a material body. When the living entity is covered by the mode of ignorance, he does not understand the individual living being and the supreme living being, and his mind is subjugated to fruitive activity. Therefore, until one has love for God, he is certainly not delivered from having to accept a material body again and again." *(Bhāg.* 5.5.4–6)

But becoming free from the cycle of birth and death requires more than just theoretical understanding. *Jñāna,* or knowledge that one is not the material body but a spirit soul, is not sufficient for liberation. One must *act* on the platform of spirit soul. This is called devotional service, which includes many practical techniques for becoming free from karma and reincarnation.

1. The first principle of devotional service is that one should always chant the Hare Kṛṣṇa mantra, Hare Kṛṣṇa, Hare Kṛṣṇa, Kṛṣṇa Kṛṣṇa, Hare Hare/ Hare Rāma, Hare Rāma, Rāma Rāma, Hare Hare.

2. One should also regularly study the Vedic literatures, especially the *Bhagavad-gītā* and *Śrīmad-Bhāgavatam,* in order to develop a thorough understanding of the nature of the self, the laws of karma, the process of reincarnation, and the means for becoming self-realized.

3. One should eat only spiritualized vegetarian foods. In the *Bhagavad-gītā* Lord Kṛṣṇa says that one should eat only food that is offered to Him in sacrifice; otherwise, one will become implicated in the reactions of karma.

patraṁ puṣpaṁ phalaṁ toyaṁ
yo me bhaktyā prayacchati
tad ahaṁ bhakty-upahṛtam
aśnāmi prayatātmanaḥ

"If one offers Me with love and devotion a leaf, a flower, a fruit, or water, I will accept it." (Bg. 9.26) It is clear from this verse that the Lord is not interested in offerings of liquor, meat, fish, or eggs but wants simple vegetarian foods prepared with love and devotion.

We should reflect on the fact that food cannot be produced by men working in factories. Men cannot eat gasoline, plastic microchips, or steel. Food is produced by the Lord's own natural arrangements, and offering food to Kṛṣṇa is a form of recognizing our debt to God. How does one offer food to Kṛṣṇa? The technique is very simple and easy to perform. Anyone may keep a small altar in his home or apartment, with a picture of Lord Kṛṣṇa and the spiritual master on it. The simplest form of offering is to place the food before the pictures and say, "My dear Lord Kṛṣṇa, please accept this humble offering," and chant Hare Kṛṣṇa. The key to this simple process is devotion. God is hungry not for our food but for our love, and eating this purified food that has been accepted by Kṛṣṇa frees one from karma and inoculates one against material contamination.

4. The positive principle of offering vegetarian food to Kṛṣṇa automatically includes the negative principle of avoiding meat, fish, and eggs. Eating meat means participating in the business of unnecessarily killing other living beings. This leads to bad karmic reactions in this life or the next. The laws of karma state that if one kills an animal to eat it, then in his next life the killer will also be killed and eaten. There is also karma involved in taking the lives of plants, but this is negated by the process of offering the food to Kṛṣṇa, because He says He will accept such vegetarian offerings. One should also give up intoxicants, including coffee, tea, alcohol, and tobacco. Indulging in intoxication means associating with the mode of ignorance and may result in one's taking a lower birth in the next life.

5. Other techniques for becoming free from the cycle of reincarnation include offering the fruit of one's work to God. Everyone must work for simple bodily sustenance, but if work is performed only for one's own satisfaction, one must accept the karmic results and receive good and

bad reactions in future lives. The *Bhagavad-gītā* warns that work must be performed for the satisfaction of the Lord. This work, known as devotional service, is karma-free. Working in Kṛṣṇa consciousness means sacrifice. The human being *must* sacrifice his time or money for the satisfaction of the Supreme. "Work done as a sacrifice for Viṣṇu [Kṛṣṇa] has to be performed; otherwise work causes bondage in this material world." (Bg. 3.9) Work performed as devotional service not only saves one from karmic reaction but gradually elevates one to transcendental loving service of the Lord—the key to entering the kingdom of God.

It is not necessary to change one's occupation. One may be a writer and write for Kṛṣṇa, an artist and paint for Kṛṣṇa, a cook and cook for Kṛṣṇa. Or, if one is not able to directly engage one's talents and abilities in serving Kṛṣṇa, one may sacrifice the fruits of one's work by contributing a portion of one's earnings to help propagate Kṛṣṇa consciousness throughout the world. One should, however, always earn one's living by honest means. For example, one should not work as a butcher or gambler.

6. Parents must raise their children in God consciousness. The *Vedas* state that parents are responsible for the karmic reactions of their children. In other words, if your child incurs bad karma, you must suffer some of that karma yourself. Children should be instructed about the importance of obeying God's laws and avoiding sinful behavior and should be taught how to develop love for the Supreme Lord. And parents should make them thoroughly familiar with the subtle laws of karma and reincarnation.

7. Kṛṣṇa conscious persons should not engage in illicit sex, i.e., sex outside of marriage or sex not for the purpose of conceiving a child. It should also be noted that abortion carries a special karmic reaction—those who participate in killing unborn children may be placed in the womb of

a mother who chooses abortion and themselves be slaughtered in the same horrible way. But if one agrees to no longer commit such sinful acts, one can become freed from karmic reaction by inoffensive devotional chanting of the holy names of God.

8. One should regularly associate with people who are trying to become free from the influence of karma and who are attempting to break out of the cycle of birth and death. Because they are living in harmony with the spiritual principles governing the universe, devotees of Lord Kṛṣṇa become transcendental to the influence of material nature and begin to display genuine spiritual characteristics. So just as one can contract a disease by associating with a sick person, one can gradually reawaken one's own transcendental qualities by associating with Kṛṣṇa's devotees.

By following these simple techniques, anyone can become free from the effects of karma. Conversely, one who does not follow them is sure to become entangled in the actions and reactions of material life. The laws of nature are very strict, and unfortunately, most people are unaware of them. But ignorance of the law is no excuse. One who is arrested for speeding will not be excused if he tells the judge that he was not aware of the speed limit. If a person is ignorant of the principles of hygiene, nature will not excuse him from incurring disease. And if a child ignorant of the nature of fire sticks his hand into one, he must be burned. Therefore, to free ourselves from the endless repetition of birth and death, we must understand the laws of karma and reincarnation. Otherwise, we will have to come back to this material world again and again; and we must remember that we may not always return as human beings.

The soul in its conditioned state perpetually travels through time and space. By the cosmic law of karma, it takes up residence in different bodies on different planets within the material universes. But wherever the soul journeys, it encounters the same conditions. As Lord Kṛṣṇa says in the *Bhagavad-gītā* (8.16): "From the highest planet in the material world down to the lowest, all are places of misery wherein repeated birth and death take place. But one who attains to My abode . . . never takes birth again." The *Gītā* and other Vedic literatures are instruction manuals that teach us the real goal of life's journey. By understanding the science of reincarnation, we can free ourselves from the forces of karma and return to the antimaterial regions of knowledge, bliss, and eternity.

His Divine Grace A.C. Bhaktivedanta Swami Prabhupāda

His Divine Grace A. C. Bhaktivedanta Swami Prabhupāda appeared in this world in 1896 in Calcutta, India. He first met his spiritual master, Śrīla Bhaktisiddhānta Sarasvatī Gosvāmī, in Calcutta in 1922. Bhaktisiddhānta Sarasvatī, a prominent religious scholar and the founder of sixty-four Gauḍīya Maṭhas (Vedic institutes), liked this educated young man and convinced him to dedicate his life to teaching Vedic knowledge. Śrīla Prabhupāda became his student and, in 1933, his formally initiated disciple.

At their first meeting, in 1922, Śrīla Bhaktisiddhānta Sarasvatī requested Śrīla Prabhupāda to broadcast Vedic knowledge in English. In the years that followed, Śrīla Prabhupāda wrote a commentary on the *Bhagavad-gītā,* assisted the Gauḍīya Maṭha in its work, and, in 1944, started *Back to Godhead,* an English fortnightly magazine. Single-handedly, Śrīla Prabhupāda edited it, typed the manuscripts, checked the galley proofs, and even distributed the individual copies. The magazine is now being continued by his followers.

In 1950 Śrīla Prabhupāda retired from married life, adopting the *vānaprastha* (retired) order to devote more time to his studies and writing. He traveled to the holy city of Vṛndāvana, where he lived in humble circumstances in the historic temple of Rādhā-Dāmodara. There he engaged for several years in deep study and writing. He accepted the renounced order of life (*sannyāsa*) in 1959. At Rādhā-Dāmodara, Śrīla Prabhupāda began work on his life's masterpiece: a multivolume commentated translation of the eighteen-thousand-verse *Śrīmad-Bhāgavatam* (*Bhāgavata Purāṇa*). He also wrote *Easy Journey to Other Planets.*

After publishing three volumes of *Śrīmad-Bhāgavatam,* Śrīla Prabhupāda came to the United States, in September 1965, to fulfill the mission of his spiritual master. Subsequently, His Divine Grace wrote more than fifty volumes of authoritative commentated translations and summary studies of the philosophical and religious classics of India.

When he first arrived by freighter in New York City, Śrīla Prabhupāda was practically penniless. Only after almost a year of great difficulty did he establish the International Society for Krishna Consciousness, in July of 1966. Before he passed away on November 14, 1977, he had guided the Society and seen it grow to a worldwide confederation of more than one hundred *āśramas,* schools, temples, institutes, and farm communities.

In 1972 His Divine Grace introduced the Vedic system of primary and secondary education in the West by founding the *gurukula* school in Dallas, Texas. Since then his disciples have established similar schools throughout the United States and the rest of the world.

Śrīla Prabhupāda also inspired the construction of several large international cultural centers in India. At Śrīdhāma Māyāpur, in West Bengal, devotees are building a spiritual city centered on a magnificent temple—an ambitious project for which construction will extend over many years to come. In Vṛndāvana are the Kṛṣṇa-Balarāma Temple and International Guesthouse, *gurukula* school, and Śrīla Prabhupāda Memorial and Museum. There are also major temples and cultural centers in Mumbai, New Delhi, Baroda, Tirupati, Ahmedabad, Siliguri, and Ujjain.

Other centers are planned in many important locations on the Indian subcontinent.

Śrīla Prabhupāda's most significant contribution, however, is his books. Highly respected by scholars for their authority, depth, and clarity, they are used as textbooks in numerous college courses. His writings have been translated into over fifty languages. The Bhaktivedanta Book Trust, established in 1972 to publish the works of His Divine Grace, has thus become the world's largest publisher of books in the field of Indian religion and philosophy.

In just twelve years, despite his advanced age, Śrīla Prabhupāda circled the globe fourteen times on lecture tours that took him to six continents. In spite of such a vigorous schedule, Śrīla Prabhupāda continued to write prolifically. His writings constitute a veritable library of Vedic philosophy, religion, literature, and culture.

Glossary

A

Ācārya—a spiritual master who teaches by example.

Ahiṁsā—nonviolence.

Āśrama—the residence of persons practicing spiritual life.

B

Bhadrakālī—a name of the demigoddess Durgā, the personified material energy.

Bhagavad-gītā—the paramount scripture of the Vedic tradition, embodying the teachings of Lord Kṛṣṇa to His devotee Arjuna and expounding devotion to the Supreme Lord as both the principal means and the ultimate end of spiritual perfection.

Bhakti-yoga—the yoga system of practicing devotional service to the Supreme Lord, Kṛṣṇa.

Brāhmaṇa—the intelligent class of men, according to the system of social and spiritual orders.

C

Caitanya Mahāprabhu—the incarnation of the Supreme Lord disguised as His own devotee, who descended to teach love of God through the process of congregational chanting of the holy names of the Lord.

Caitanya-caritāmṛta—Kṛṣṇadāsa Kavirāja Gosvāmī's presentation of the life and philosophy of Lord Caitanya Mahāprabhu.

D

Deja-vu—the feeling of having already experienced a present situation.

Demigods—living beings empowered by the Supreme Lord to supervise the material universe.

Devotional service—the process of lovingly offering all of one's activities for the pleasure of the Supreme Lord.

G

Ganges—a sacred river that flows from the lotus feet of Lord Viṣṇu.

Goodness—the mode of material nature characterized by sense control and spiritual enlightenment.

Gross body—the outer covering of the conditioned soul, composed of the tangible physical elements.

Guru—a spiritual master.

H

Hare—One of the seed words of the Hare Kṛṣṇa mantra; the vocative form of Harā, the supreme pleasure energy of God, which can bring the conditioned soul into contact with Kṛṣṇa.

I

Ignorance—the mode of material nature characterized by madness, illusion, and sleep.

Impersonalism—the doctrine that falsely holds that personality is ultimately an illusion.

J

Jñāna—theoretical knowledge.

K

Kālī—the personified material energy of the Lord.

Karma—activity in the material world, which always entangles one in some reaction, whether good or bad.

Karmātmaka—one whose mind is entangled in material desires and activities.

Kṛṣṇa—the Supreme Personality of Godhead in His original, two-armed form. He is the origin of all of the Lord's other forms and incarnations.

L

Liberated soul—one who is freed from identification with the material body and mind.

Living entity—the soul.

M

Mahā-mantra—the great chanting for deliverance:
Hare Kṛṣṇa, Hare Kṛṣṇa, Kṛṣṇa Kṛṣṇa, Hare Hare
Hare Rāma, Hare Rāma, Rāma Rāma, Hare Hare

Mahārāja—a king.

Mantra—a combination of transcendental sounds that has the effect of purifying one's consciousness of material contamination.

Material body—a temporary form composed of physical elements that covers the conditioned soul.

Material desires—the propensity to control and exploit the physical elements for one's own satisfaction.

Material world—the part of creation where repeated birth and death take place.

Māyā—illusion; forgetfulness of one's relationship with Kṛṣṇa.

Meditation—the process of concentrating one's mind for the purpose of self-realization.

Modes of nature—the three divisions of the Lord's material energy, namely goodness, passion, and ignorance.

N

Nārāyaṇa—a name of the four-handed expansion of the Supreme Lord, Kṛṣṇa.

P

Parsees—members of the Zoroastrian religious sect in India.

Passion—the mode of material nature characterized by intense pursuit of mundane goals.

Purāṇas—the eighteen texts expounding the teachings of the *Vedas* through historical and allegorical narrations.

R

Rāma—a name of the Supreme Personality of Godhead meaning "the source of all pleasure."

Reincarnation—the passage of the soul at the time of death from one material body to another.

Ṛg Veda—one of the four divisions of the original *Veda.*

S

Saṁsāra—the cycle of birth and death.

Sanskrit—the classical literary language of ancient India.

Self-realization—the process of understanding the soul to be different from the body.

Soul—an eternal, conscious particle of the Lord's spiritual energy.

Spiritual master—one who awakens the original, eternal consciousness of the living entity.

Spiritual world—that part of the creation characterized by eternality, knowledge, and bliss.

Śravaṇa—the process of hearing about the Supreme Lord.

Śrīmad-Bhāgavatam (Bhāgavata Purāṇa)—Vyāsadeva's "spotless *Purāṇa,*" which deals exclusively with pure devotional service to the Supreme Lord.

Subtle body—the inner covering of the conditioned soul, composed of mind, intelligence, and false ego.

Supersoul—the localized aspect of the Supreme Lord, present in the hearts of all living beings.

T

Transcendental knowledge—the correct understanding of the soul and its relationship with the Supreme Lord, Kṛṣṇa.

Transmigration—*See:* Reincarnation

U

Upaniṣads—the philosophical division of the *Vedas,* meant for bringing the student closer to understanding the personal nature of the Absolute Truth.

V

Vedas—the sacred scriptures of ancient India.

Viṣṇu—a name of the Supreme Personality of Godhead as the creator and maintainer of the material universes.

Viṣṇudūtas—the servants of Lord Viṣṇu.

Voidism—the concept that everything is ultimately illusory or nonexistent.

Y

Yamadūtas—the servants of Yamarāja.

Yamarāja—the demigod in charge of punishing the sinful after death. He is also recognized as one of the chief authorities on devotional service to Lord Kṛṣṇa.

Yoga—the process of controlling the mind and senses for the purpose of self-realization and ultimately God realization.

Yogī—one who is striving in one of the yoga processes.

Sanskrit Pronunciation Guide

The system of transliteration used in this book conforms to a system that scholars have accepted to indicate the pronunciation of each sound in the Sanskrit language.

The short vowel **a** is pronounced like the **u** in b**u**t, long **ā** like the **a** in f**a**r. Short **i** is pronounced as in p**i**n, long **ī** as in p**i**que, short **u** as in p**u**ll, and long **ū** as in r**u**le. The vowel **ṛ** is pronounced like the **ri** in **ri**m, **e** like the **ey** in th**ey**, **o** like the **o** in g**o**, **ai** like the **ai** in **ai**sle, and **au** like the **ow** in h**ow**. The *anusvāra* (**ṁ**) is pronounced like the **n** in the French word *bo***n**, and *visarga* (**ḥ**) is pronounced as a final **h** sound. At the end of a couplet, **aḥ** is pronounced **aha**, and **iḥ** is pronounced **ihi**.

The guttural consonants—**k, kh, g, gh,** and **ṅ**—are pronounced from the throat in much the same manner as in English. **K** is pronounced as in **k**ite, **kh** as in Ec**kh**art, **g** as in **g**ive, **gh** as in di**g h**ard, and **ṅ** as in si**ng**.

The palatal consonants—**c, ch, j, jh,** and **ñ**—are pronounced with the tongue touching the firm ridge behind the teeth. **C** is pronounced as in **ch**air, **ch** as in staun**ch-h**eart, **j** as in **j**oy, **jh** as in he**dgeh**og, and **ñ** as in ca**ny**on.

The cerebral consonants—**ṭ, ṭh, ḍ, ḍh,** and **ṇ**—are pronounced with the tip of the tongue turned up and drawn back against the dome of the palate. **Ṭ** is pronounced as in **t**ub, **ṭh** as in ligh**t-h**eart, **ḍ** as in **d**ove, **ḍh** as in re**d-h**ot, and **ṇ** as in **n**ut. The dental consonants—**t, th, d, dh,** and **n**—are pronounced in the same manner as the cerebrals, but with the forepart of the tongue against the teeth.

The labial consonants—**p, ph, b, bh,** and **m**—are pronounced with the lips. **P** is pronounced as in **p**ine, **ph** as in u**ph**ill, **b** as in **b**ird, **bh** as in ru**b-h**ard, and **m** as in **m**other.

The semivowels—**y, r, l,** and **v**—are pronounced as in **y**es, **r**un, **l**ight, and **v**ine respectively. The sibilants—**ś, ṣ,** and **s**—are pronounced, respectively, as in the German word *s*prechen and the English words **sh**ine and **s**un. The letter **h** is pronounced as in **h**ome.

The International Society for Krishna Consciousness
Founder-*Ācārya:* His Divine Grace A.C. Bhaktivedanta Swami Prabhupāda

CENTERS AROUND THE WORLD

Partial List

CANADA

Brampton, Ontario — 6 George Street South, 2nd Floor, L6Y 1P3/ Tel. (416) 648-3312/ iskconbrampton@gmail.com
Calgary, Alberta — 313 Fourth St. N.E., T2E 3S3/ Tel. (403) 265-3302/ vamanstones@shaw.ca
Edmonton, Alberta — 9353 35th Ave. NW, T6E 5R5/ Tel. (780) 439-9999/ edmonton@harekrishnatemple.com
Montreal, Quebec — 1626 Pie IX Boulevard, H1V 2C5/ Tel. & fax: (514) 521-1301/ iskconmontreal@gmail.com
◆ **Ottawa, Ontario** — 212 Somerset St. E., K1N 6V4/ Tel. (613) 565-6544/ radha_damodara@yahoo.com
Regina, Saskatchewan — 1279 Retallack St., S4T 2H8/ Tel. (306) 525-0002 Or -6461/ jagadishadas@yahoo.com
Scarborough, Ontario — 3500 McNicoll Avenue, Unit #3, M1V 4C7/ Tel. (416) 300 7101/ iskconscarborough@hotmail.com
◆ **Toronto, Ontario** — 243 Avenue Rd., M5R 2J6/ Tel. (416) 922-5415/ toronto@iskcon.net
◆ **Vancouver, B.C.** — 5462 S.E. Marine Dr., Burnaby V5J 3G8/ Tel. (604) 433-9728/ akrura@krishna.com/ Govinda's Bookstore & Cafe: (604) 433-7100 or (888) 433-8722

RURAL COMMUNITY

Ashcroft, B.C. — Saranagati Dhama (mail: P.O. Box 99, V0K 1A0)/ Tel. (250) 457-7438/ iskconsaranagati@hotmail.com

U.S.A.

Atlanta, Georgia — 1287 South Ponce de Leon Ave., N.E., 30306/ Tel. & fax: (404) 377-8680/ admin@atlantaharekrishnas.com
Austin, Texas — 10700 Jonwood Way, 78753/ Tel. (512) 835-2121/ sda@backtohome.com
Baltimore, Maryland — 200 Bloomsbury Ave., Catonsville, 21228/ Tel. (410) 744-1624/ contact@iskconbaltimore.org
Berkeley, California — 2334 Stuart Street, 94705/ Tel. (510) 540-9215/ info@iskconberkeley.net
Boise, Idaho — 1615 Martha St., 83706/ Tel. (208) 344-4274/ boise_temple@yahoo.com
Boston, Massachusetts — 72 Commonwealth Ave., 02116/ Tel. (617) 247-8611/ info@iskconboston.org
◆ **Chicago, Illinois** — 1716 W. Lunt Ave., 60626/ Tel. (773) 973-0900/ chicagoiskcon@yahoo.com
Columbus, Ohio — 379 W. Eighth Ave., 43201/ Tel. (614) 421-1661/ premvilasdas.rns@gmail.com
◆ **Dallas, Texas** — 5430 Gurley Ave., 75223/ Tel. (214) 827-6330/ info@radhakalachandji.com
◆ **Denver, Colorado** — 1400 Cherry St., 80220/ Tel. (303) 333-5461/ info@krishnadenver.com
Detroit, Michigan — 383 Lenox Ave., 48215/ Tel. (313) 824-6000/ gaurangi108@hotmail.com
Gainesville, Florida — 214 N.W. 14th St., 32603/ Tel. (352) 336-4183/ kalakantha.acbsp@pamho.net
Hartford, Connecticut — 1683 Main St., E. Hartford, 06108/ Tel. & fax: (860) 289-7252/ pyari108@gmail.com
◆ **Honolulu, Hawaii** — 51 Coelho Way, 96817/ Tel. (808) 595-4913/ narahari@hawaiiweddings.com
Houston, Texas — 1320 W. 34th St., 77018/ Tel. (713) 686-4482/ management@iskconhouston.org
Kansas City, Missouri — Rupanuga Vedic College, 5201 Paseo Blvd., 64110/ Tel. (816) 924-5640/ rvc@rvc.edu
Laguna Beach, California — 285 Legion St., 92651/ Tel. (949) 494-7029/ info@lagunatemple.com
Las Vegas, Nevada — Govinda's Center of Vedic India, 7181 Dean Martin Dr., 89118/ Tel. (702) 434-8332/ info@govindascenter.com
◆ **Los Angeles, California** — 3764 Watseka Ave., 90034/ Tel. (310) 836-2676/ membership@harekrishnala.com
◆ **Miami, Florida** — 3220 Virginia St., 33133 (mail: 3109 Grand Ave., #491, Coconut Grove, FL 33133/ Tel. (305) 442-7218/ devotionalservice@iskcon-miami.org
Mountain View, California — 1965 Latham St., 94040/ Tel. (650) 336 7993 / isvtemple108@gmail.com
New Orleans, Louisiana — 2936 Esplanade Ave., 70119/ Tel. (504) 304-0032 (office) or (504) 638-1944 (temple)/ gopal211@aol.com
New York, New York — 305 Schermerhorn St., Brooklyn, 11217/ Tel. (718) 855-6714/ ramabhadra@aol.com
New York, New York — The Bhakti Center, 25 First Ave., 10003/ Tel. (212) 253-6182
Orlando, Florida — 2651 Rouse Rd., 32817/ Tel. (407) 257-3865/ info@iskconorlando.com
Philadelphia, Pennsylvania — 41 West Allens Lane, 19119/Tel. (215) 247-4600/ info@iskconphiladelphia.com
Philadelphia, Pennsylvania — 1408 South St., 19146/ Tel. (215) 985-9303/ govindasvegetarian.gmailcom
Phoenix, Arizona — 100 S. Weber Dr., Chandler, 85226/ Tel. (480) 705-4900/ premadhatridd@gmail.com
Portland, Oregon — 2095 NW Aloclek Dr., Suites 1107 & 1109, Hillsboro 97124/ Tel. (503) 675-5000/ info@iskconportland.com
◆ **St. Louis, Missouri** — 3926 Lindell Blvd., 63108/ Tel. (314) 535-8085 or 255-2207/ root@iskconstlouis.org

◆ Temples with restaurants or dining

Salt Lake City, Utah — 965 E. 3370 South, 84106/ Tel. (801) 487-4005/ utahkrishnas@gmail.com
San Diego, California — 1030 Grand Ave., Pacific Beach, 92109/ Tel. (858) 483-2500/ krishna.sandiego@gmail.com
Seattle, Washington — 1420 228th Ave. S.E., Sammamish, 98075/ Tel. (425) 246-8436/ info@vedicculturalcenter.org
◆ **Spanish Fork, Utah** — Krishna Temple Project & KHQN Radio, 8628 S. State Road, 84660/ Tel. (801) 798-3559/ utahkrishnas@gmail.com
Tallahassee, Florida — 1323 Nylic St., 32304/ Tel. & fax: (850) 224-3803/ tallahassee.iskcon@gmail.com
Towaco, New Jersey — 100 Jacksonville Rd. (mail: P.O. Box 109), 07082/ Tel. & fax: (973) 299-0970/ madhupati.jas@pamho.net
◆**Tucson, Arizona** — 711 E. Blacklidge Dr., 85719/ Tel. (520) 792-0630/ sandaminidd@cs.com
Washington, D.C. — 10310 Oaklyn Dr., Potomac, Maryland 20854/ Tel. (301) 299-2100/ info@iskconofdc.org

RURAL COMMUNITIES

Alachua, Florida (New Raman Reti) — 17306 N.W. 112th Blvd., 32615 (mail: P.O. Box 819, 32616)/ Tel. (386) 462-2017/ alachuatemple@gmail.com
Carriere, Mississippi (New Talavan) — 31492 Anner Road, 39426/ Tel. (601) 749-9460 or 799-1354/ talavan@hughes.net
Gurabo, Puerto Rico (New Govardhana Hill) — Carr. 181, Km. 16.3, Bo. Santa Rita, Gurabo (mail: HC-01, Box 8440, Gurabo, PR 00778)/ Tel. & fax: (787) 767-3530 or 737-1722/ manoratha@gmail.com
Hillsborough, North Carolina (New Goloka) — 1032 Dimmocks Mill Rd., 27278/ Tel. (919) 732-6492/ bkgoswami@earthlink.net
◆ **Moundsville, West Virginia (New Vrindaban)** — 3759 McCrearys Ridge Rd., 26041/ Tel. (304) 843-1600 (Guesthouse extension: 111)/ mail@newvrindaban.com
Mulberry, Tennessee (Murari-sevaka) — 532 Murari Lane, 37359 Tel. (931) 759-6888/ murari_sevaka@yahoo.com
Port Royal, Pennsylvania (Gita Nagari) — 534 Gita Nagari Rd., 17082/ Tel. (717) 527-4101/ dhruva.bts@pamho.net
Sandy Ridge, North Carolina (Prabhupada Village) — 1283 Prabhupada Rd., 27046/ Tel. (336) 593-2322/ prabhupadavillage@gmail.com

ADDITIONAL RESTAURANTS

Hato Rey, Puerto Rico — Tamal Krishna's Veggie Garden, 131 Eleanor Roosevelt, 00918/ Tel. (787) 754-6959/ tkveggiegarden@aol.com

UNITED KINGDOM AND IRELAND

Belfast, Northern Ireland — Brooklands, 140 Upper Dunmurray Lane, BT17 OHE/ Tel. +44 (028) 9062 0530/ hk.temple108@gmail.com
Birmingham, England — 84 Stanmore Rd., Edgbaston B16 9TB/ Tel. +44 (121) 420 4999/ iskconbirmingham@gmail.com
Cardiff, Wales — The Soul Centre, 116 Cowbridge Rd., Canton/ Tel. +44 (29) 2039 0391/ the.soul.centre@pamho.net
Coventry, England — Kingfield Rd., Coventry (mail: 19 Gloucester St., Coventry CV1 3BZ)/ Tel. +44 (24) 7655 2822 or 5420/ haridas.kds@pamho.net
Dublin, Ireland — 83 Middle Abbey St., Dublin 1/ Tel. +353 (1) 661 5095/ dublin@krishna.ie; Govinda's: info@govindas.ie
Leicester, England — 21 Thoresby St., North Evington, LE5 4GU/ Tel. +44 (116) 276 2587/ pradyumna.jas@pamho.net
Lesmahagow, Scotland — Karuna Bhavan, Bankhouse Rd., Lesmahagow, Lanarkshire, ML11 0ES/ Tel. +44 (1555) 894790/ karunabhavan@aol.com
◆ **London, England (city)** — 10 Soho St., W1D 3DL/ Tel. +44 (20) 7437-3662; residential /pujaris, 7439-3606; shop, 7287-0269; Govinda's Restaurant, 7437-4928/ london@pamho.net
◆ **London, England (country)** — Bhaktivedanta Manor, Dharam Marg, Hilfield Lane, Watford, Herts, WD25 8EZ/ Tel. +44 (1923) 851000/ info@krishnatemple.com; (for accommodations:) bmguesthouse@krishna.com
London, England (south) — 42 Enmore Road, South Norwood, SE25 5NG/ Tel. +44 7988857530/ krishnaprema89@hotmail.com
London, England (Kings Cross) — 102 Caledonian Rd., Kings Cross, Islington, N1 9DN/ Tel. +44 (20) 7168 5732/ foodforalluk@aol.com
Manchester, England — 20 Mayfield Rd., Whalley Range, M16 8FT/ Tel. +44 (161) 226-4416/ contact@iskconmanchester.com
Newcastle-upon-Tyne, England — 304 Westgate Rd., NE4 6AR/ Tel. +44 (191) 272 1911
◆ **Swansea, Wales** — 8 Craddock St., SA1 3EN/ Tel. +44 (1792) 468469/ iskcon.swansea@pamho.net; restaurant: govin-das@hotmail.com

RURAL COMMUNITIES

London, England — (contact Bhaktivedanta Manor)
Upper Lough Erne, Northern Ireland — Govindadwipa Dhama, Inisrath Island, Derrylin, Co. Fermanagh, BT92 9GN/ Tel. +44 (28) 6772 1512/ iskconbirmingham@gmail.com

ADDITIONAL RESTAURANTS

Dublin, Ireland — Govinda's, 4 Aungier St., Dublin 2/ Tel. +353 (1) 475 0309/ info@govindas.ie
Dublin, Ireland — Govinda's, 83 Middle Abbey St., Dublin 1/ Tel. +353 (1) 661 5095/ info@govindas.ie
Dublin, Ireland — Govinda's, 18 Merrion Row, Dublin 2/ Tel. +353 (1) 661 5095/ praghosa.sdg@pamho.net

AUSTRALASIA

AUSTRALIA

Adelaide — 25 Le Hunte St. (mail: P.O. Box 114,

Kilburn, SA 5084)/ Tel. & fax: +61 (8) 8359-5120/ iskconsa@tpg.com.au
Brisbane — 32 Jennifer St., Seventten Mile Rocks, QLD 4073 (mail: PO Box 525, Sherwood, QLD 4075)/ Tel. =61 (7) 3376 2388/ info@iskcon.org.au
Canberra — 44 Limestone Ave., Ainslie, ACT 2602 (mail: P.O. Box 1411, Canberra, ACT 2601)/ Tel. & fax: +61 (2) 6262-6208
Melbourne — 197 Danks St. (mail: P.O. Box 125), Albert Park , VIC 3206/ Tel. +61 (3) 9699-5122/ melbourne@pamho.net
Perth — 155–159 Canning Rd., Kalamunda (mail: P.O. Box 201 Kalamunda 6076)/ Tel. +61 (8) 6293-1519/ perth@pamho.net
Sydney — 180 Falcon St., North Sydney, NSW 2060 (mail: P.O. Box 459, Cammeray, NSW 2062)/ Tel. +61 (2) 9959-4558/ admin@iskcon.com.au
Sydney — Govinda's Yoga and Meditation Centre, 112 Darlinghurst Rd., Darlinghurst NSW 2010 (mail: P.O. Box 174, Kings Cross 1340)/ Tel. +61 (2) 9380-5162/ sita@govindas.com.au

RURAL COMMUNITIES

Bambra, VIC (New Nandagram) — 50 Seaches Outlet, off 1265 Winchelsea Deans Marsh Rd., Bambra VIC 3241/ Tel. +61 (3) 5288-7383
Cessnock, NSW (New Gokula) — Lewis Lane (off Mount View Rd., Millfield, near Cessnock (mail: P.O. Box 399, Cessnock, NSW 2325)/ Tel. +61 (2) 4998-1800/
Murwillumbah, NSW (New Govardhana) — Tyalgum Rd., Eungella (mail: P.O. Box 687), NSW 2484/ Tel. +61 (2) 6672-6579/ ajita@in.com.au

RESTAURANTS

Brisbane — Govinda's, 99 Elizabeth St., 1st floor, QLD 4000/ Tel. +61 (7) 3210-0255
Brisbane — Krishna's Cafe, 1st Floor, 82 Vulture St., West End, QLD 4000/ brisbane@pamho.net
Burleigh Heads — Govindas, 20 James St., Burleigh Heads, QLD 4220/ Tel. +61 (7) 5607-0782/ ajita@in.com.au
Maroochydore — Govinda's Vegetarian Cafe, 2/7 First Avenue, QLD 4558/ Tel. +61 (7) 5451-0299
Melbourne — Crossways, 1st Floor, 123 Swanston St., VIC 3000/ Tel. +61 (3) 9650-2939
Melbourne — Gopal's, 139 Swanston St., VIC 3000/ Tel. +61 (3) 9650-1578
Newcastle — 110 King Street, NSW 2300/ Tel. +61 (02) 4929-6900/ info@govindascafe.com.au
Perth — Govinda's Restaurant, 194 William St., Northbridge, W.A. 6003/ Tel. +61 (8) 9227-1648/ perth@pamho.net
Perth — Hare Krishna Food for Life, NSW 2300/ Tel. +61 (02) 4929-6900/ info@govindascafe.com.au

NEW ZEALAND AND FIJI

Auckland, NZ — The Loft, 1st Floor, 103 Beach Rd./ Tel. +64 (9) 3797301
Christchurch, NZ — 83 Bealey Ave. (mail: P.O. Box 25-190)/ Tel. +64 (3) 366-5174/ Fax: +64 (3) 366-1965/ iskconchch@clear.net.nz
Hamilton, NZ — 188 Maui St., RD 8, Te Rapa/ Tel. +64 (7) 850-5108/ rmaster@wave.co.nz
Labasa, Fiji — Delailabasa (mail: P.O. Box 133)/ Tel. +679 812912
Lautoka, Fiji — 5 Tavewa Ave. (mail: P.O. Box 125)/ Tel. +679 666 4112/ regprakash@excite.com
Nausori, Fiji — Hare Krishna Cultural Centre, 2nd Floor, Shop & Save Building 11 Gulam Nadi St., Nausori Town (mail: P.O. Box 2183, Govt. Bldgs., Suva)/ Tel. +679 9969748 or 3475097/ Fax: +679 3477436/ vdas@frca.org.fj
Rakiraki, Fiji — Rewasa (mail: P.O. Box 204)/ Tel. +679 694243
Sigatoka, Fiji — Queens Rd., Olosara (mail: P.O. Box 1020)/ Tel. +679 6520866 or 6500349/ drgsmarna@connect.com.fj
Suva, Fiji — 166 Brewster St. (mail: P.O. Box 4229, Samabula)/ Tel. +679 331 8441/ Fax: +679 3100016/ iskconsuva@connect.com.fj
Wellington, NZ — 105 Newlands Rd., Newlands/ Tel. +64 (4) 478-4108/ info@iskconwellington.org.nz
Wellington, NZ — Bhakti Lounge, 1st Floor, 175 Vivian St, Te Aro Tel. +64 (4) 801-5500/ yoga@bhaktilounge.org.nz

RURAL COMMUNITY

Auckland, NZ (New Varshan) — Hwy. 28, Riverhead, next to Huapai Golf Course (mail: R.D. 2, Kumeu)/ Tel. +64 (9) 412-8075/ Fax: +64 (9) 412-7130

RESTAURANTS

Auckland, NZ — The Loft Yoga Lounge, 1st Floor, 103 Beach Rd./ Tel. +64 (9) 3797301/ theloft.akld@gmail.com
Wellington, NZ — Higher Taste Hare Krishna Restaurant, Old Bank Arcade, Ground Flr., Corner Customhouse, Quay & Hunter St., Wellington/ Tel. +64 (4) 472-2233/ Fax: (4) 472-2234/ highertaste@iskconwellington.orgorg.nz

Far from a center?

Call us at: 1-800-927-4152. Or contact us on the Internet.

---

http://www.krishna.com
E-mail: bbt.usa@krishna.com

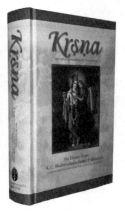